Chaos of War
Balance of Life

A SOLDIER'S JOURNAL FROM AFGHANISTAN

WILL HIGGINBOTHAM

Names listed in this journal by the first initial only are for those whose consent was not obtained.

Chaos of War, Balance of Life: A Soldier's Journal from Afghanistan

Published by Wheatmark®
1760 East River Road, Suite 145, Tucson, Arizona 85718 USA
www.wheatmark.com

ISBN: 978-1-62787-114-3
LCCN: 2014935217

INTRODUCTION

When you read this, you will laugh; you might cry, but do so knowing that this part of my life is over. Good or bad, it is finished. Now the only thing to do is maintain faith and seek balance. —Will

THIS JOURNAL AND ARTWORK are dedicated to all veterans (past, present, and future), with special recognition for those who gave all. And also for those who suffered battle wounds and scarring that may or may not be visible to the naked eye.

This is the sharing of one sergeant's story and experiences throughout his deployment in Afghanistan. Vivid emotions that he could not share with his men, instead, were shared with me—his mom. The artwork dispersed throughout the journal was drawn by him at various times in his life, not all in Afghanistan.

It was my son's hope and prayer that this journal would be used for good. For veterans who need to know that they are not alone in their feelings and thoughts experienced during and after war. For new soldiers who have not yet experienced wartime. For families and friends of veterans who want to know what their soldier may have experienced but who do not want to pry into that part of their life.

This will be an emotional journey for the reader. It is haunting and powerful and may bring tears to your eyes.

I thank you for honoring the memory of my son, Sergeant William Henry Higginbotham III of the 173rd Airborne Combat

Brigade, 2-503rd Scouts, by reading this book. During wartime, he was known affectionately as Higg or Hippie. After wartime, he wanted to be called Will. His mantra throughout his time at home was "Life is good." He would often say, "Life without challenge is a farce." His wish for this world was that all people could live in peace.

My son died tragically in a helicopter crash in May of 2013. Prior to his death, he had begun the journey to publish this journal that he wrote for me while he was serving in Afghanistan. To honor my son, who I feel gently nudging at my heart; I am finishing that journey for him.

I pray God's richest blessings be upon each veteran and current member of our military. I pray that He will place a hedge of protection around those who are serving America on a battlefield anywhere in this world.

Matthew 5:9, "Blessed are the peacemakers."

–Terri Kennedy
Will's mother

Ma,

I hope to give this to you when I finish it. If I don't finish filling the pages for whatever reason, know what I have drawn is for you, and the blank pages were intended for you. I love you, Mom.

Love,
W

LEONARDO
STUDY OF
THE HEAD
OF CHRIST
FOR THE
LAST SUPPER

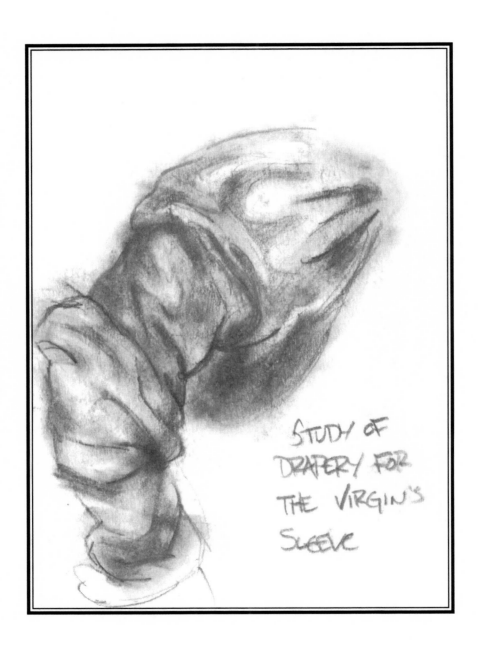

STUDY OF
DRAPERY FOR
THE VIRGIN'S
SLEEVE

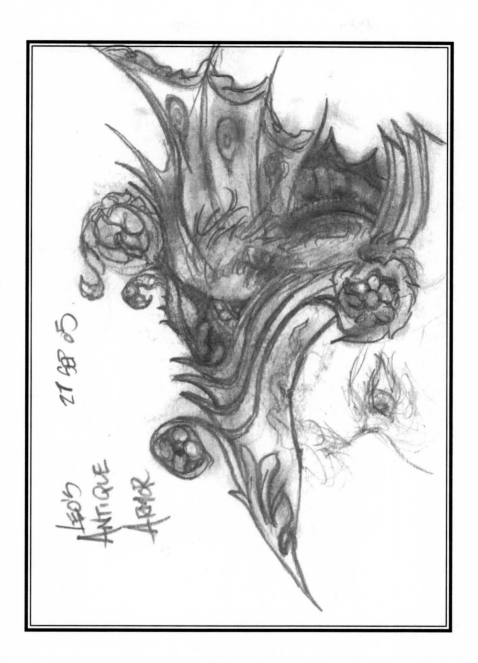

LEO'S
ANTIQUE
ARMOR

21 SEP 05

7

HUNTER KILLER
TEAM 2
2-503 SCOUTS

Don't march to the beat of another drum.
Someone else may hear the beat.
Instead, choose another path.
THINK and put headphones on.

Cycle

SUA SPONTE

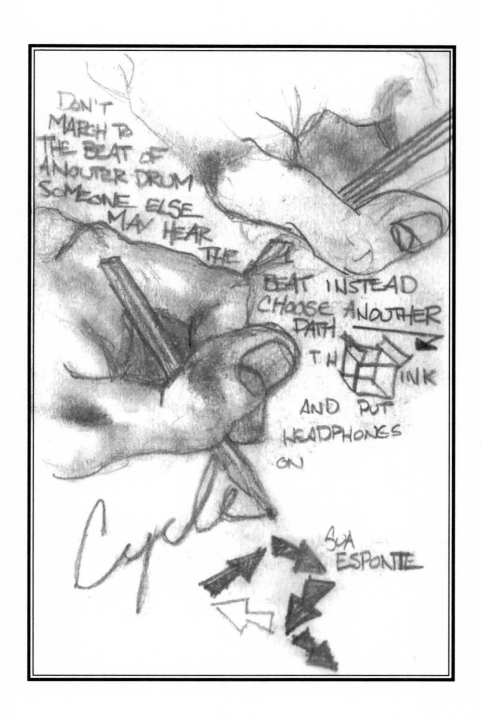

11

Soldiers are not unlike the knives they carry. Honed and sharp but carrying scars on its edge from battle. The handle worn and smoothed from dirt cemented into fabric with sweat and blood.

It remembers its role, as it can never forget how at times life finds itself balancing and ending on its point. It is used as a tool in the never-ending and always-shifting means to no end battle. Soldiers, while your knives are needed in your hands, stay like your blade—cold, sharp. Carry no regret. It will end. One day.

SOLDIERS ARE NOT UNLIKE
THE KNIVES THEY CARRY.
HONED AND SHARP BUT
CARRYING SCARS ON IT'S
EDGE FROM BATTLE.
THE HANDLE WORN   WITH
AND SMOOTHED   SWEAT
FROM DIRT   AND
                        BLOOD,
CEMENTED   IT REMEMBERS
INTO   IT'S ROLE
FABRIC   AS IT CAN NEVER
                   FORGET HOW AT
                  TIMES LIFE FINDS
                IT'S SELF BALANCING
             AND ENDING ON IT'S
           POINT. IT IS USED AS
          A TOOL IN THE NEVER
        ENDING AND ALWAYS SHIFTING
       MEANS TO NO END BATTLE.
      SOLDIERS, WHILE YOUR KNIFE IS
NEEDED IN YOUR HAND STAY LIKE
YOUR BLADE, COLD, SHARP CARRY
NO REGRET. IT WILL END. ONE DAY.

28 Sep 05

Mom,

I had another idea. Since I've been gone I have missed out on a lot of talks with you, so I figure I will share some with you through this book.

Tomorrow we go to hunt mercenaries. I hate mercs.

They are well armored and have an extremely dangerous motivation: greed. These dudes are bad. I've fought them a few times in the past. They fight like us but with less patience. That's how we succeed against them: patience.

Why am I telling you these things? Well, I will only either give this book to you in person or have one of my men mail it to you should God take me. So either way, you shouldn't be able to worry about me from this.

28 SEP 05

Mom,
I had another idea, since
I've been gone & have missed
out on a lot of talk
with you so I figure I
will share some with you
though this book.
        Tomorow we go to hunt
Arab and Chezchvian
Mercinaries. I hate these
they are well armed and have an
extremely dangerous motivation, greed.
These dudes are bad, I've fought them
a few times in the past. They
fight like us but with less patience.
That's how we succeed against them,
patience.
        Why I am telling you these
things, well I will only either
give this book to you in person
or have one of my men mail it
to you should God take me.
So either way you shouldn't be
able to to worry about me from this.

15

So the idea is [that] I get to write you all the things you worry about but don't know exactly why.

This is one story I have to share because it has haunted me since it happened, and I fear I will never find peace from it.

[Around] June 5 we were scrambled to provide relief for Battle Company when they came under fire in the Arghandab Valley just outside of a small village named Solan. This is a place nightmares are made of. A jungle-like orchard [covers] the valley floor—mostly poppy fields and marijuana fields with thousands of fruit trees and various vines and vegetable-bearing plants. This part of the valley is fairly narrow and the walls aren't that steep. Huge granite boulders make caves and holes anyone could hide in.

Our helicopter banked hard right. I saw ten to twelve men running from the boulders carrying RPK machine guns, RPGs, and assault rifles. The bird came in fast and landed. I could hear the bullets snap past us. They clipped the rotors and the body [of the helicopter]. Thankfully, it wasn't God's plan to put a bullet in the engine. That is never a good time. The bird dropped us off. The dust from the brown out gave us enough concealment to find cover behind some rocks. We dropped one [merc] when he tried shooting at us. Me, Scott, and Josh assembled and moved to the building the Taliban were running out of and into the rocks. The building was a mosque they had turned into a bomb factory. That meant the whole village was enemy. We already knew that, but that confirmed it. That meant the village elders allowed them to use the mosque. Bad deal. We moved from the building to the rocks. I'm going into detail because if I write it to you, it's like I'm telling you. It gets it off my chest. We killed three more working up the valley. Two of them were already wounded.

But we put them down because they were still a threat. Execution of necessity. That's what it was. The Army calls it clearing the objective. The third [man] was on the high ground running for a cave. I shot him in the back of the head. He died after about a minute of screaming through his throat and what was left of his jaw. We were ordered to continue to clean. I continued on point, trying to keep my men far enough back and to the side [so that] I would be the first to spot any more enemy. We stopped at a steep wall. I scanned the area. I looked to my left and visually cleared the ground between me and McD (Josh); as I looked, I saw no threat. I turned to look toward Sprague (Scott). As I turned, something caught my eye. Twelve inches from me where I had just looked, a man was swinging a rifle; the sun caught the rifle and the reflection caught my eye. I shot him once in the chest and once in the face. Then I walked over to him and put six more rounds in him to confirm it. He had the drop on me. I have nightmares about that day. After I killed the last [merc], we were called to pull back. We bounded back at a high rate of speed. When we got back to the mosque, an attack helicopter showed up and turned the objective into an ashtray. We were extracted after dark. We waited for the sun to set in an apple orchard. We ate crab apples to build our strength and pass the time. I lit a cigarette. Scott said, "Those things will kill you." We laughed. The brigade and battalion sgt. majors met us when we got back. They shook our hands and took a picture with us. Three against twelve. That's what they put us against. Bastards.

First time I've told that story. Until you read this, I think only me and God will know how close it came that day. I can still see their faces and feel the sweat burn my eyes. I cry and don't know why. I think I'm so overloaded, the emotion creeps out in a few quiet sobs as tears hit the floor.

I want to leave this place here but I don't think I ever can. There [are] so many stories like that one. I don't know if I should, but I think I will write them down. So tonight I'll sleep. Or try to, anyway. Tomorrow we will hunt the mercs. One day I will rest. But not for a while.

In this moment I do feel peace. I think that's why I don't want to put my pen down.

Lord, forgive me of my sins
Give me strength in weakness
Endurance in fatigue and
Clarity in chaos
Keep my hands solid and my feet swift
Help me destroy the evil to protect the innocent
Give us rest in sleep and keep us in the night
Bring my men home before myself
Give our loved ones peace
Thank you for giving me another
Day and help me through tomorrow

Your son, W
That's the prayer I've said and will say every night. Good night, Mom.

—all my love

PROTECT US THIS
I PRAY...

29 Sep 05

They are the cause of this ...

The American government has declared war on terrorism. OK, in doing so. They have collected a handful of allies: NATO, other powerful countries with interest. And, oh yeah, don't forget Afghan drug lords. They sit with each other discussing the future to protect [their] interests.

Because we can't burn down opium fields, drug lords can sell heroin to wherever, including America. That money, some of it goes to Al-Qaeda brethren who in turn can buy mercenaries and weapons to aid in the jihad (holy war) the Taliban has against coalition forces. The Taliban buys outstanding weapons like 54-7s or heat-seeking missiles at a mere twenty thousand dollars per shot. Those missiles are used to do things like shoot down CH-47 helicopters, much like the one that was hit three days ago, killing five men. Their bodies were shredded and spread all over the side of a mountain. My Scout team was tasked in securing the remains. Trying to match body parts with body sizes on men you once ate dinner with. Trying to remember who was married so you can get the hand with its owner. They give you a list so you can match pant sizes with top sizes when the body is not connected.

They are responsible. They kill. Soldiers are expendable. I know it; I've seen it. We go to war and die, not what anyone wants to happen, but nonetheless that is how it works. They know it. They know the evil they sit at dinner with. Damn them. Damn them for damning us. Not a good day.

Thank you, Lord, for giving me another day, and help me get through tomorrow.

So much hate. So much death. So much killing.

I love you, Mom. I just wish we were Swiss. They have the right idea: neutrality in world affairs.

What Will Your Son Become?

I enjoy teaching.
I enjoy art.
I like to build things and work with my hands.
I like children.
I like to climb.
I enjoy danger to a point.
I am a man of God, although maybe not an ideal one.
I want a family. Children.
I want love in my house and peace in its walls.
I can barely remember peace or freedom.
Yeah, that's it.
I will become a bum.
My life's ambition: BUMHOOD

Here's a drawing of me using age progression of 30 years. I know
there is a striking resemblance to my current profile, but just
imagine how accurate it will be when I'm old.

Places I've Been

Home	Syria	In Iraq for the fall of Baghdad
Alaska	Turkey	The northern assault into Iraq and the May 3 Riots.
Hawaii	Ireland	I've climbed the highest peaks in
Okinawa	Tajikistan	the Swiss, French Swiss, Italian
Thailand	Afghanistan	Swiss, and German Swiss Alps. I've
Australia	Pakistan	seen the midnight sun in Alaska
Canada	Switzerland	and the oceans of the world. I am
Mexico	France	truly blessed.
Italy	Spain	
Austria	The Vatican	
Germany	Romania	
Kuwait	Holland	
Iraq	Kurdistan	

Self portrait
with fat head.
15 APR 02

23

Cage in a Bird

The caged bird's song can bring a prideful man easily to his knees. The reason is simple. Pride is the man's cage. When he hears the bird's song, he realizes he is not in the cage; the cage is in him. Lord, let me not have pride to a fault.

These colors don't run...
They bleed instead
LOST

One thing Love

If the world could possess one trait in every creature from men to mice, love would be the answer that would fix all.

SOMETIMES THE SIMPLE CAN BE THE EXACT OPPOSITE

One thing... Love

If the World could passes one trait in every creature from men to mice love would be the answer that would fix all.

SOMETIMES THE SIMPLE CAN BE THE EXACT OPPOSITE

BROKEN

Random
Implosion

When the sky falls, where will you hide?

No Home

When an animal is caged, all of what he knew is lost only in a matter of time. They lose survival traits.

A cheetah, when placed in a walled refuge, will stop running as a pastime. It will do what it was born to do only [because of] the pain [that] hunger brings. Never forget.

WHEN AN ANIMAL IS CAGED ALL OF
WHAT HE KNEW IS LOST IN THE
ONLY MATTER OF TIME. THEY
LOSE
SURVIVAL
TRAITS.
A CHEETAH
WHEN
PLACED
IN A
WALLED
REFUGE
WILL
STOP
RUNNING
AS A
PAST TIME. IT WILL DO WHAT IT
WAS BORN TO DO FOR THE
ONLY REASON BEING THE PAIN
HUNGER BRINGS. NEVER FORGET.

JAILED.

FREEDOM

How many times can you perform the same task without forming patterns? Patterns...

I think about too many pointless things. I cannot wait to turn off the switch from war and live, just live.

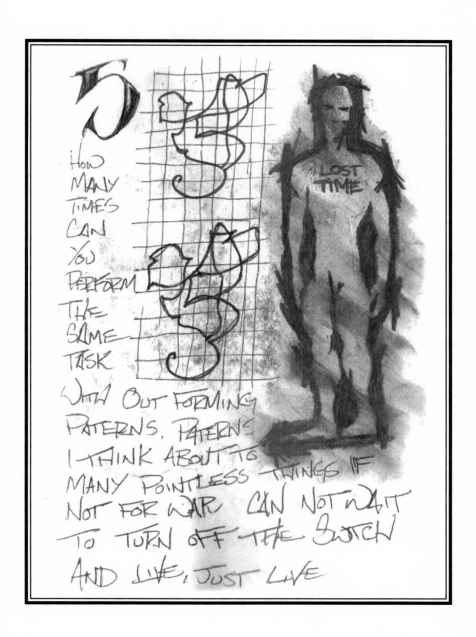

5

How
MANY
TIMES
CAN
YOU
PERFORM
THE
SAME
TASK
WITH OUT FORMING
PATERNS. PATERNS
I THINK ABOUT TO
MANY POINTLESS THINGS IF
NOT FOR WAR. CAN NOT WAIT
TO TURN OFF THE SWITCH
AND LIVE, JUST LIVE

LOST
TIME

Horse's Head
5 Oct. 05
Time is so very slow.

When I rise up, let it be graceful like a bird.
When I fall, let it be without regret
Like a leaf.
—KS

God, show me the way; the devil is trying to break me.
Jesus, walk with me; I'm living in hell.
I know I have angels watching me from the other side.
Please, Father, forgive me for trying to buy freedom
in the eyes of men.

The answer for prayers unprayed brings a light in the night. A boulder in the middle of a field and a voice on the phone from the other side of the world when the last thing expected from a day of pain and loss was love. Thank you.

When I rise up let it be graceful like a bird. When I fall let it be without regret like a leaf.

—K.S.

GOD SHOW ME THE WAY THE DEVIL IS TRYING TO BREAK ME. JESUS WALK WITH ME, I'M LIVING IN HELL, I KNOW I HAVE ANGELS WATCHING ME FROM THE OTHER SIDE. PLEASE FATHER FORGIVE ME FOR TRYING TO BUY FREEDOM IN THE EYES OF MEN

THE ANSWER FOR PRAYERS UNPRAYED BRINGS A LIGHT IN THE NIGHT. A BOULDER IN THE MIDDLE OF A FIELD, AND A VOICE ON THE PHONE FROM THE OTHER SIDE OF THE WORLD WHEN THE LAST THING EXPECTED FROM A DAY OF PAIN AND LOSS WAS LOVE. THANK YO..

Hawks: They find a lifemate and live, hunt, and reproduce with the one creature made for them. Independent and enduring in all things. If I could be most like any of God's creatures, make me like the hawk.

FLY, DIVE, SOAR, GLIDE

Lord, let me soar among the ones who can not be here now. When I die, give me wings before my soul returns to you so I can soar over those I must leave behind. Amen.

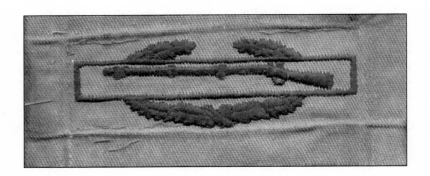

12 Oct

Days drag on as time continues to show its impervious way of turning days into night before they have the opportunity to come back around again. The evenings are cool, almost chilled. Winter will be here soon, if it's not already and just biding its time to smile as it brings its white-gray insanity. So many questions I try to answer with one response. It is His will why one man dies and another lives. This war, this illusion of democracy, is the reason we die in deserts and mountains even the inhabitants choose not to care about. America is an idea, a concept at best; it's not a geographic location. When someone is lost, are they really lost, or is it that they just think they are?

As words fill pages and lines form drawings, time is passing. Five months. Everyone says time will go by fast. In their reality I'm sure it does; in mine I think it chooses not to. Boredom, funeral/memorial services, killing, thinking about killing, and trying to dream those I love into reality are the building blocks of my present life. I do not want to be remembered through medals and patches or the sound rifles make when fired in unison. I do not want this place, this hate, to be the last thing I see through mortal eyes. There are too many things I want to do before this life is finished. I want to be a father and a good man to my wife. I want to be a solid fixture and acting role in my family. I want to be physically, mentally, and spiritually healthy. Only five months and these pages, words, pictures, and drawings, along with a few scars, will be the only tangible proof I was ever here. If I should die, please don't remember me as a soldier; remember me as your loving son.

Bernini's David. My favorite statue.

It's the moment David is throwing a stone. Focus, poise, clarity, and confidence.

Seeing the statue in person was a definitive point in my life.

15 Oct

And what if Jesus said, "I am not in buildings of wood and stone. Split a piece of wood and I am there. Move a rock and you will find me."

My favorite time to see Renaissance or Roman structures is late at night when it's still dark, just before dawn.

I've walked through Rome seeing the monuments with a bottle of wine and no crowds. Peace where there is normally commotion. I think it is tranquil.

15 OCT

LONDON, WESTMINSTER ABBEY

AND WHAT IF JESUS SAID, "I AM NOT IN BUILDINGS OF WOOD AND STONE. ~~THROUGH~~ SPLIT A PIECE OF WOOD AND I AM THERE MOVE A ROCK AND YOU WILL FIND ME.

My favorite time to see renaissance or roman structures is late at night when it's still dark just before dawn. I've walked through Rome seeing the monuments with a bottle of wine and no crowds. Peace where there is normally commotion & think it's tranquil

45

Here's a concept... What if there were no churches? What if, instead of investing billions of dollars into buildings, all the tithes and offerings went directly to helping people? No earthly reward besides the gratitude that comes with helping fellow man. Services could be held in an open field or in the yard of the faith's leader. How many of the world's problems could be solved, if any? That's the problem. We are so focused on religion and new places of worship and how to earn money to build a church that we lose sight of our spirituality. I have felt closer to God on top of a mountain than [I] ever [have] in a church. So many places you can go and feel God's love from the surroundings alone. I have felt the spirit in churches all over the world, but it was caused by the congregation, not the construction. I know my way of thinking is far from the general church-going population's way, but maybe that is part of the reason I know I will never quite feel like I can belong to your average church-going population. I don't walk a higher path. I think maybe I'm just looking for a different one.

How I see a quaint village.

River, deltas, mosques, and wells imperative to know and observe. Known to throw ordinance in wells. Bomb factories in mosques and attack when they are praying or washing feet to pray.

Neutralize a threat before it becomes a threat. Stay off roads. IEDs in roads.

Two terrain features between you and well and enemy. Three between extraction HLZ and enemy. Snipers acquire and neutralize targets so the assaulting force has minimal opposition. One shot. One kill. RECON!!!

HOW I SEE A QUIANT VILLAGE. RIVER DELTAS MOSQUES AND WELLS IMPARITIVE TO KNOW & OBSERVE. KNOWN TO THROW ORDANANCE. IN WELLS BOMB FACTORIES IN MOSQUES AND ATTACK WHEN THEY ARE PRAYING OR WASHING FEET TO PRAY. NEUTRALIZE A THREAT BEFORE IT BECOMES A THREAT. STAY OFF ROADS. IED'S IN ROADS. 2 TERRAIN FEATURES BETWEEN YOU AND ENEMY 3 BETWEEN EXTRACTION HLZ & ENEMY. SNIPERS AQUIRE & NEUTRALIZE TARGETS SO THE ASSULTING FORCE HAS MIN. OPPISITION. ONE SHOT ONE KILL. RECON!!!

17 Oct

Believe it or not I have studied a little since I've been in the army. I like to [study] artist[s]. Bernini is my favorite sculptor. He will take something perfect and not try and change it but add a new dimension to it.

[Other famous sculptors would] take perfection and try to put a twist on it to make it theirs.

17 OCT Believe it or not
I have studied a little
since I've been in the
Army.
I like
to take
an
artist.
Bernini
is my
favorite
sculpter.
He will
take
something
perfect
and not
try and
change
it but
add a
new
dimension
to it.
Raphael
took perspective
and tried
to put a
twist on it
to make
it his

TOMB OF LORENZO
DE' MEDICI
FLORENCE ITALY
STANZA DELLA SEGNATURA
BEAUTY
REVEALED TRUTH   -AIR
     -FIRE   POETRY -
THEOLOGY   APOLLO-MARSYAS
ORIGINAL SIN   (MYTHOLOGY DISPUTE)
DISPUTE (DISPUTE)   PARNASSUS
                    AUGUSTUS AND THE
RATIONAL TRUTH   AENEID
     -WATER   ALEXANDER AT THE
PHILOSPHY   TOMB OF
PRIMUM MOBILE (HIGH SCHOOL) ACHILLES
     SCHOOL OF ATHENS
          (UNIVERSITY)
GOODNESS -EARTH JUSTICE, JUDGMENT
OF SOLOMON, FORTITUDE, PRUDENCE, TEMPER-
ANCE, JUSTINIAN, GREGORY IX

51

Bernini never did that. He would just amplify an aspect enough to where it would bring a form of light to the art.

Michelangelo was my favorite painter because his work reflects his life...oppression. Leonardo was the great inventor. This guy's mind was literally fifteen hundred years ahead of his time. Well, maybe five hundred years, anyway. Back to studying. I've studied the events that took place in their times. I've realized people think and worry way too much. They need to experience more. Let go of what we know and try to find more.

Bernini never did that
he would just amplify
an aspect enough to
where it would bring a
form of light to
the art. Michael
was my favorite
artist because
his work reflects
his life... oppression
Leonardo the great
inventor. This
guy's mind was
literally 1,500
years ahead of
his time well
maybe 500 years
anyway. Back
to studying. I've studied
the events and ways
of thinking that took
place in their time. I've
realized people think and
worry way to much they need
to experience more. Let go of
what we know and try to
find more.

As it comes it goes. Is this necessary? Violence is a quick [fix], but is it needed? Is it possible for the endless words of politicians to ever be used to stop what they are constantly trying to prevent? Or will they remain worthless in the peace the world I fear will never embrace? Sometimes I wish we would be subjected to a worldwide disaster. Not that I want to see destruction. I would just like to challenge the people of the world [so that] they would have no choice but to depend on each other.

Freedom, truth, health, art, life, peace,
love, help, balance, equality
Vs.
War, hate, violence, aggression, attack, kill,
death, pain, misery, end.

As it comes it goes. ~~Is~~ Is this necessary. Violence is a quick resolve but is it needed. Is it possible for the endless words of politicians to ever be used to stop what they are constantly trying to prevent. Or will they remain worthless in the peace the world I fear will never embrace. Sometimes I wish we would be subjected to a world dilemma. Not that I want to see destruction I would just like to challenge the people of the world to where they would have no choice but to depend on each other.

FREEDOM
TRUTH
HEALTHY
AT LIFE
PEACE LOVE
HELP BALANCE
EQUALITY

WAR
HATE
VIOLENCE
AGGRESSION
ATTACK
KILL
DEATH
PAIN
MISERY
END

AVE GRATIA PLENA

ANGEL OF THE ANNUNCIATION TITIAN

ANGELS KEEP US SAFE SAVE US FROM THE ENEMY AND OURSELVES. IN A BATTLE OR FIRE FIGHT OR WHAT EVER THEY HAVE AND WILL CALL ALTERCATIONS WHERE MAN KILLS MAN, THERE IS AN OUTSIDE FORCE THAT GUIDES OUR HANDS AND WEAPONS ALLOWING THE ONLY LIVES TO BE TAKEN ARE THOSE THAT ARE NECASSARY. THANK YOU FOR NOT ALLOWING US TO KILL OUT OF RAGE. BELIEVE ANGELS ARE PRESENT WHEN WE LAUGH AND CRY.

Angels keep us safe. Save us from the enemy and ourselves. In a battle or firefight or whatever they have and will call altercations where man kills man. There is an outside force that guides our hands and weapons, allowing the only lives to be taken [to be] those that are necessary. Thank you for not allowing us to kill out of rage.

I believe angels are present when we laugh and cry.

58

I believe in saints and angels, demons, and ghosts. I believe they are among us. I have seen demons in men. I have seen acts no man of his own will could carry out. I believe I have been tormented by demons in my sleep and I still am. They can strike fear, hate, and resentment into any man's soul if only for a short time. I believe I have encountered angels. I believe there have been times the only reason I have lived was through the guidance of angels. I believe in saints—men who are so spiritually close to the Lord they are on a higher level of the same plane shared by all mortals. I do not believe in some beliefs that certain men are a link between humans and God. I do not believe a man can call for a penance to be paid for the saving of one's soul. I believe God is embraced in many forms by many people around the world. I believe about 70 percent of the Bible is what makes up the truth. I believe in the time from when Jesus was a boy to the time he became a man is not in the Bible because he lived. By lived I mean he did things that young men do that mothers are "concerned" about. If a child read in the Bible that Jesus didn't make his bed, the rules would change. These are things that I have come to realize; I don't know if they are fact and I will not try to instill these beliefs in anyone. I believe every person has the privilege of coming to their own conclusions. I do not believe in war. I believe in times of war killing cannot be avoided. I do not believe in killing children, women, or men. I believe once a person chooses to fight they are no longer people; they are combatants, targets. I have killed combatants of all ages. I pray the Lord will forgive me and help me to continue to live without regret. I also pray He will give me peace from what I have done in times of war. I believe in living free and dying well. I believe in fighting for the preservation of life and the right to freedom. I do not believe in killing for oil or fighting for medals. Lord, give me peace and help me sleep tonight.

This is one of Michelangelo's unfinished sculptures intended to be placed in the front room near the tomb of Lorenzo. So much work put into this one piece for it to be left unfinished. I guess in life that is just the way it works out sometimes.

The men who have died here—God be with their families. Help bring closure to the things unfinished.

This is one of Michealango's unfinished sculptures intended to be placed in the front room near the tomb of Lorenzo so much work put into this to be one left piece unfinished for it I guess in life that is. just the way it works out some time. The men who have died here God be with their families. Help bring closer to the things unfinished

19 Oct 2005

Bernini's David—

This is hands down my favorite freestanding single piece of sculpture. He took Michelangelo's David and broke the mold. He brought it to life. His ability to capture expression is amazing. I hope to be able to make a piece of art that someone can relate to the way that I relate to this.

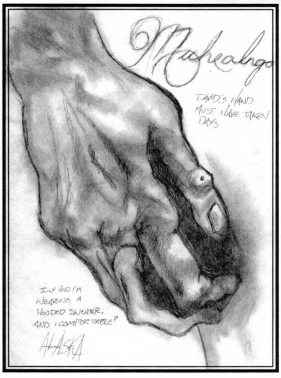

DAVID'S HAND
MUST HAVE TAKEN
DAYS

JULY AND I'M
WEARING A
HOODED SWEATER-
AND I COMFORTABLE?

Mom,

This is one of my favorite places I've ever been. It is also the place where I plan on proposing to my girlfriend.

The plan is I take her through the streets of Rome, have an excellent dinner, and take a bottle of wine and show her Rome at night. After, I'll take her to Trevi Fountain, wait for everyone to leave, and when we're alone I'll tell her the story about Roman soldiers who, before they left for war, would throw coins in the fountain to help ensure their safe return home and to the ones they loved. That's the same thing I did with my girlfriend in my mind before I came here. After I tell her that, I'm going to pull out the ring and tell her something like, "I don't know if you want to throw this in or not, but I do want you to dip it in the water if you'll marry me." That way there's no yes or no. There's an action, a meaning, an act. So now you know the plan. Whether or not it happens that way, because no plans ever really work out, is up to chance. But know I have a plan. Mom, if you can keep it a secret, I would appreciate it.

This was intended to be Aaron. Unfortunately it turned out more like one of the characters from the musical *Cats*. Well, I guess sometimes art is hit or miss, and this time I think it's more of a miss. So I guess this is art striking out. [I] should maybe use erasers again.

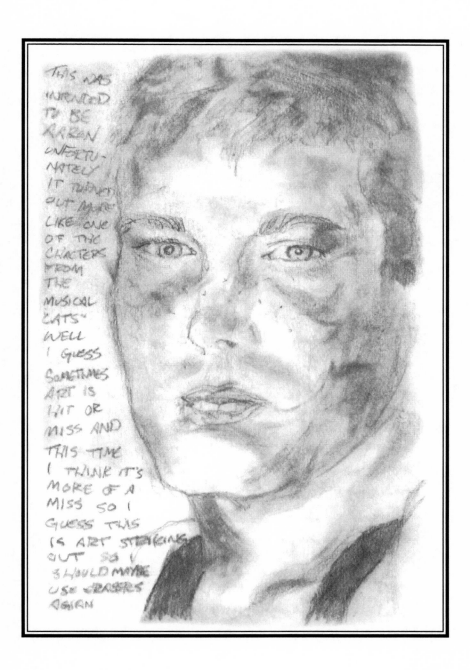

THIS WAS
INTENDED
TO BE
RARUN
UNFORTU-
NATELY
IT TURNED
OUT MORE
LIKE ONE
OF THE
CHARACTERS
FROM
THE
MUSICAL
"CATS"
WELL
I GUESS
SOMETIMES
ART IS
HIT OR
MISS AND
THIS TIME
I THINK IT'S
MORE OF A
MISS SO I
GUESS THIS
IS ART STINKING
OUT SO I
SHOULD MAYBE
USE ERASERS
AGAIN

22 Oct 05
Leave Lagham FOB Wolverine

23 Oct 05
Wolverine to Sweeney to Atghar to Sweeney to Shinkay

25 Oct 05
Shinkay toHarnay to Lagham.

Going to the Pakistan border near Atghar. Staying the night in FOB. Leaving FOB at dawn [for] Lagham every morning to go to next sight. Three nights [and] four days of driving when all this could be done in one day by helicopter. IEDs on every road.

Stupid mission.

The Solder with a Broken Heart

He loves his home as he made a promise.
Dimly, yellow-lit lights and fog
Make up the first memories of his new life.

Running from the past, he is stranded in the present.
He's been around the world,
He's seen many things,
And, now he prays for the future to bring
A stop to the present,
For a wish of tomorrow.

So many friends have passed,
So many lives have finished.
When the sun sets, it ends a day
Far changed from when it rose.
Was life ever simple,
Can it ever be simple?
So much in him has been altered,
So many views changed.
Bag Pipes play at the ceremony.
Coffins pass as he renders his salute.
They return home now,
They know peace.

A clinched fist and a weapon,
The only two things I can see.
I kill the man staring straight through me,
Not much effort does it take.
Another life has come to an end,
A man with no name is all I can bring with me.
4 men dead
3 in the water

The stream runs red.
Helicopters fly over,
The world stops,
The heart races,
Pride is felt because lives were saved.
Humanity has been taken, what's left is jade.
The world speeds up,
The heart slows down.

Her voice allows me rest,
Puts to sleep the chaos of the day.
The day is finished but not over.
It stretches and contours,
Time is nonexistent,
It holds no truth:
It only contains reality.
A loved one lies
Sick with cancer,
The end is near.
She is a mother,
More than a friend.
Why must her life
Be near its end?
She is so close to my heart.

When this is over,
Can it ever be finished?
This is all in view
I wish it were over.
Power breeds hate.
Hate results in war.
War is bought with blood.
Blood is cashed in with money.
Money creates power.

No matter what those with power say,
It will never be finished.
It can never be over.
The truth is:
This life is what I hate,
More than war,
More than those who end life.
The participation of it
Slowly kills me,
A piece at a time.
Left in the earth,
What is left when it's stripped away,
When who we think we are, is gone?
What can be salvaged?
Is there nothing to rescue,
Or am I rescuing nothing?

Finally near the end:
Still so far from home.
I lie awake feeling so desperately alone.
I know in spirit,
So many are helping me deal with it.
So close to the end.
Yet so ready to break,
I just have to keep this path straight.
The wounded go home.
The dead have moved on.
As I sit here still waiting,
Waiting for dawn.

I will be ok,
As I always am.
It just gets me,
If I'll ever know who I truly am:
A man or a boy,
A lion or a mouse,
A lover or a warrior?
I think in moderation,
I am all these things.
Just waiting to be born with wings.
So I wait, as I always have.
I'll be ok.
Right now I'm just sad.

Tonight we prep,
Tomorrow we hunt.
In between is the part,
Where the pains fill my heart.
Tempers are short.
As thumbs itch,
We grow tired.
We need new things.
We need to see color.
Surrounded by tan, brown, and grey.

ANGER FEAR HATE LOVE LUST COMPASSION MERCY NO
MERCY KILL DON'T KILL HUNT HUNTED LIFE DEATH
BIRTH LOVE PEACE REST SLEEP

24 Aug 05

21 Oct 05

THE HUNT

Men, you are going into hell. This is not the place for the weak. If you cannot do this, if you cannot control the fire in your blood, leave now. No questions, no second chances. If you choose to get on these helicopters, know you are going to a place where men will kill and men will die. You may bleed today. No matter what happens or where you find yourself, always keep these facts in mind. If you die, you are going to a far better place, and you will finally know the peace you have fought for. If you live, always remember we leave no one behind, and no man walks alone. See you all on the other side.

28 Oct:
Happy Halloween in three days.
Things I Fear

- needles
- mosquitos with malaria
- IEDs (pressure plated without command detonators)
- Losing my left hand
- Ravine ambushes against us
- NOT MAKING IT TO THANKSGIVING
- Camel spiders

ARGHANDAB VALLEY

A week 'til Halloween. We're at Wolverine. We stayed in Sweeney last night. May have to drive to Golahan tomorrow. Really don't want to drive through the Arghandab Valley for any reason. We've been really lucky when it comes to that place. We're the only ones in the battalion who haven't taken any casualties in that place. We did get a truck blown up there, another burned up, and yet another truck drowned in the river. We've also killed over twenty Taliban in the stretch of the valley that goes from Harray down to Spin Ghar. I just want to be finished with this place. I haven't been able to sleep much the last few nights. I think its fried nerves from driving these damned roads. No joke. You'll be driving along and start seeing chunks of HMMWV. Then you'll see a huge burnt hole in the ground. You think, "Great. That's where M. got his arm blown off." I'm so stressed out and depressed right now. My men keep me going. Without them I would have probably shot myself in the foot by now. This place is not worth it. These people, I am beginning to care less and less about them. They know how long we've been here. They also know some are beginning to pull the trigger quicker. The 508th burned those bodies because of hygiene reasons, so the stories go. The truth is a far cry from that. So this book is cool because I really feel like I am getting things off my chest when I write in it. I know through this you'll get a better idea of me. My guys, they look to me for leadership but they don't really need it; they just need a push in the right direction on occasion. I think I lean on them more than they rely on me. I call my girlfriend almost every day. I really love her. I hope we get along in person as well as we do on opposite sides of the earth; if not, we'll figure it out. Well I'm gonna count sheep. Love you.

Perfect weather today: little breeze and a cool sun. We drove the trucks from Wolverine, and now we are in a small compound in Shah Joy.

Chosen's 1st platoon is occupying it. Some good dudes out here. Very low stress actually. Kind of nice.

On occasions like this I feel secure and almost peaceful.

I get lost in music and art. I can almost forget where I am. It's quiet and the important people are gone. It's just a good break. I think I'll take a nap.

MONEY SUCKS

The root of all evil. This little concept, in my opinion, is the beginning of the end for almost all things that involve violence.

Imagine a planet where there was no money. No one had power [and] all cultures were respected and treated as equals.

I think imagining is as close as we can get to that.

I would rather live poor than die rich.

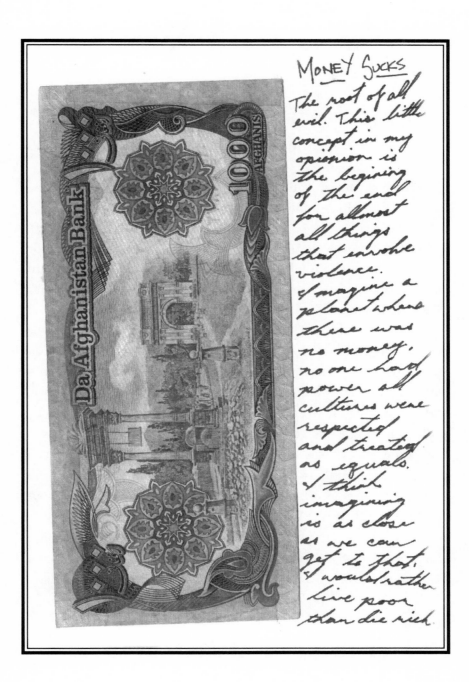

MONEY SUCKS

The root of all evil. This little concept in my opinion is the begining of the end for allmost all things that involve violence. I imagine a planet where there was no money, no one had power all cultures were respected and treated as equals. I think imagining is as close as we can get to that. I would rather live poor than die rich.

28 Oct 05

This is a 9-line. It's what we used to call the dust off helicopters in for a MEDEVAC.

This is a call I put in a couple of months ago. All three guys lived. I haven't heard much else, so I figure they must be recovering OK wherever they are or I would have heard otherwise. I am tired, Mom. I spent twelve hours on a Black Hawk for over watch while the line companies assaulted a few compounds. Sometimes it's hard to do the hard right over the easy wrong. I struggle every day with decisions I make; for example, today I let a man live. I know he was Taliban. I saw him ditch his rifle. There's a possibility he will be released on a technicality. He's the first I haven't killed in similar situations. I don't know why I didn't; I just didn't. Three other men were killed today—all Taliban. I am tired of all the blood, violence, and death. I wonder what long-term effects this life will have on my soul. I just don't want to be one of those forever-haunted men of war. Some guys just can't let go. I just want the chance to dump it all and fill the gaps with love and enlightenment. Oh well, for now I will stay sharp and cold. One day—I've been saying and thinking about "one day" quite a bit. We are on the backside of the deployment. Can't lose focus; can't get caught up in trivial BS. Well, bedtime. I almost used the S-H-I-T word in front of my mom. Good night, Ma. See you one day. Until then, thank you for your love and prayers.

Love, W

28 OCT 05

This is
a 9 line.
It is
what
we use
to call
the Dust
Off Heli-
copters
in for
medivac.
This is
a call
I put
in a
couple
of months
ago. All
3 guys

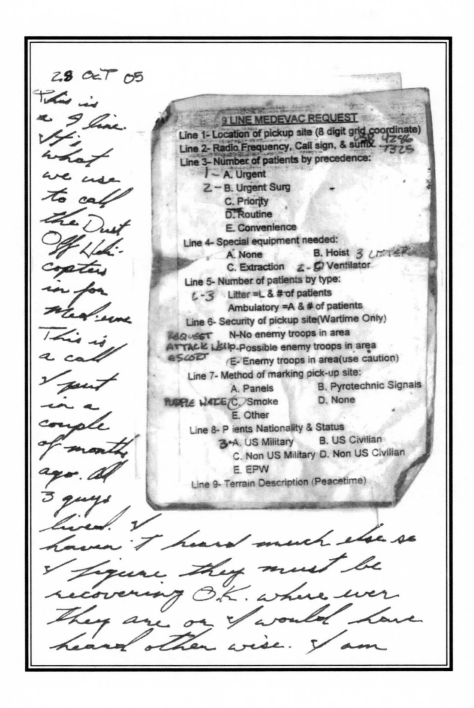

9 LINE MEDEVAC REQUEST

Line 1- Location of pickup site (8 digit grid coordinate)
Line 2- Radio Frequency, Call sign, & suffix. *4246*
7325
Line 3- Number of patients by precedence:
    1 ~ A. Urgent
    2 ~ B. Urgent Surg
    C. Priority
    D. Routine
    E. Convenience
Line 4- Special equipment needed:
    A. None   B. Hoist *3 LITTER*
    C. Extraction *2 -* D. Ventilator
Line 5- Number of patients by type:
    L-3 Litter =L & # of patients
        Ambulatory =A & # of patients
Line 6- Security of pickup site(Wartime Only)
REQUEST N-No enemy troops in area
ATTACK *HELP* P-Possible enemy troops in area
ESCORT
    E- Enemy troops in area(use caution)
Line 7- Method of marking pick-up site:
    A. Panels   B. Pyrotechnic Signals
PURPLE HAZE C. Smoke   D. None
    E. Other
Line 8- P ients Nationality & Status
    3 A. US Military   B. US Civilian
    C. Non US Military D. Non US Civilian
    E. EPW
Line 9- Terrain Description (Peacetime)

lived! I
haven't heard much else so
I figure they must be
recovering O.K. where ever
they are or I would have
heard other wise. I am

2 Nov 05

Just that much closer.

All this dashing around is almost coming to the beginning of the end. Twelve hour time difference between here and home. The exact other side of the world. I can feel the distance when I am near a phone or when I receive mail. My best friend here, Derek, killed a young boy, maybe fifteen or sixteen years old. Those are so difficult. He's having an awkward time dealing with it. It's hard because you want to let it all out but you know you can't; for the time [being] we hold on to our hate and anger. This place and our jobs are that much harder if we try to do our jobs out of love instead of hate. When the time comes, we will let it all go. But until then I figure we will just use it as fuel when the hard times get harder. I'll be OK, Mom.

2 Nov 85 just that much closer.
All this dashing around is
almost
coming
to the
beginning
of
the
end.
Thousand
times
different
between
here
and home.
The
times
other
side of the world. I
can feel the distance when
I am near a phone or when
I receive mail. My best

8 Nov 05

As I lay me down to rest
with only one book on my chest,
I'm broken and tired;
I just want sleep.
But right now there are so many
words I'll never speak.
The price is paid with so many lives lost.
I stop and wonder what man can buy for this cost.
If I don't know by now, I probably never will.
Just that thought makes my stomach turn ill.
Time ticks by as day gives way to night.
I wonder if, when I put down my rifle,
I will no longer have to fight.
I know the demons come when they think I am asleep.
So every night I pray to the Lord for my soul to keep.
I know I will never lose my grasp of fear.
I pray to make the screams stop; I will never turn to beer.
So tonight I'll drop my pen as I let rest
all the questions in my head.
And I will fall asleep, whispering my prayer safely in this bed.

13 Nov

Well, as always, time is ticking slowly by. This place is 0–60 and then 60–0 just as quick. The winter isn't far. On the ARF we went out toward Daychopan just north of Balo. Snow was on the mountaintop in the morning. After a few hours of flying around with the doors open and sleet freezing our bones, the snow crept down the mountain about two thousand feet. That puts the snow line about four thousand feet above our elevation. I expect the snow in a couple weeks. I hate snow. No, I hate the army in the snow.

On a lighter note, we're pretty sure all the enemy has E&E'd out of sector. All the villagers are being real friendly trying to play nice so they can get the food with the USA stamp on it. So I am in a constant state of trying to picture life post-army. I figure I will be in a constant state of trying to let this place go. I wonder if this place will ever leave me alone. I try to be optimistic about it, but it's hard to see the light when there's no tunnel.

OLD GLORY

Suffocated by the death grip of an idea transformed into a forced point of view. Our colors are barely seen through the violence of action found in democracy.

How I try to stay somewhat sane—let go, release.

I wish people would try to see the world from a different perspective on occasion. So many people choose to be as deep as the shallow end [of the] pool. Why? I understand how much bliss can be found in ignorance, but what is the point of being clueless? I want to consume life. I want to take it on. Imagine how free you can be if you just try. Someone once told me if you put all your problems in your fist, you will never solve anything. But if you lay your hand flat, palm up, and let your problems unravel themselves in the air, you can alleviate so much stress. I really need to figure out what is important and what isn't. I guess if I could do that my life would be almost simple.

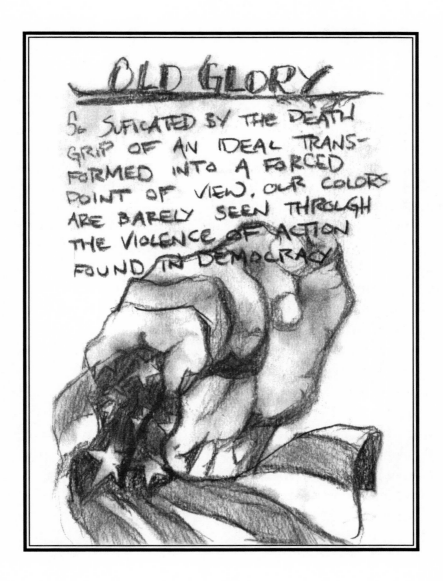

OLD GLORY

So suficated by the death grip of an ideal transformed into a forced point of view, our colors are barely seen through the violence of action found in democracy.

15 Nov 05

SYMBOLS—People see signs, ink on shins, and paint on walls. They see these images not for what they mean but for what they do or do not resemble. I am guilty of this.

I try not to hate anyone. I try not to let the cover of a book tell the story. It's so hard, Mom. I see these people, especially the ones we capture, and I want to hurt them. I want ten minutes in a room with no windows and no media, and I just want to get it all out of me. I have killed men so close, I've gotten their blood on my clothes and on my hands. I have broken arms and ribs. I have kicked another man in the face. See, and that's the thing, that's what kills my soul, even though they had weapons, even though they were combatants, they were still men; they were just pushed so far. Something in life pushes men to the point where they see the necessity to kill. I look at Iraq and this place, and the only reason I have for doing the things I've done was for the men by my side. Here's the question: what justifies us being here? 9/11? An eye for an eye? Justice? Freedom? Oil? Blood for money? Lord, forgive me. Give me peace.

SYMBOLS - People see signs, ink on skin and paint on walls, they see these images not for what they mean but what they look do not resemble. I am guilty of this.

15 NOV 05

I try not to hate anyone. I try not to let the cover of a book tell the story. It is so hard mom. I see these peole especially the ones we capture and I want to hurt them. I want 10 minutes in a room with no windows and no media and I just want to get it all out of me. I have killed men so close I've gotten

93

OPTIMISM IN THE STORM

Sometimes I just want shelter from the storm.
I pray for warmth as the rain falls.
Just a moment of peace is for what my soul calls.
Too many times my skin was weathered in nature's squalls.
Just as I think I am going to give in,
The clouds part and I feel the sun on my skin

AAARRGGGGGGGHHH!

OPTIMISIM IN THE STORM

- SOMETIMES I JUST WANT SHELTER FROM
  THE STORM
- I PRAY FOR WARMTH AS THE RAIN FALLS
- JUST A MOMENT OF PEACE IS FOR WHAT
  MY SOUL CALLS

- TO MANY TIMES MY SKIN HAS WEATHERED
  NATURES' SQUALS

- JUST AS I THINK I AM GOING TO GIVE
  IN
- THE CLOUDS PART AS I FEEL THE SUN
  ON MY SKIN

PANDORA'S
BOX

WATCH
YOUR
BACK

HEAD
DOWN
EYES
UP

17 Nov 05

I've never heard the story of St. Sebastian. I flip through my art books and see various perspectives on the day he was executed. Sometimes I truly relate to the paint on the canvas. Bound and tied to a tree to be shot with arrows.

I am under investigation yet again. This is becoming a bi-monthly event. Every instance involves me using a little thing I like to call common sense. I'm twenty-four and have about one and a half years of combat experience. I am responsible for five men. We are tight-knit and, without question, have always accomplished the mission. I have been "weathered." Now, you take our LT. He is twenty-four and is responsible for twenty men. He has four months of combat experience and has never been "in contact." Only in the military could he not only get paid twice as much as me but also be respon-sible to come up with courses of action when he has never been shot at. It's like asking a blind man to draw a picture of what he sees. Sure, he can take a swing at it, but he has never seen. He can't see what he is doing; he's lost. That's my take on young officers in the army—lost. He wanted me to drive him through an ambush site. Instead, I called helos to check the choke point. The helos found twenty "shepherds" on the valley walls. Nine against twenty, and they had the high ground. Would have been bad. So bad. All this so he could (forgive my language) "pop his cherry." Yeah, well, step off the gallows pole and move to the guillotine, please. Whatever. Just gotta get the men out of here. I'll worry about me when I get home. I can handle ignorance, just not when it comes to here.

17 NOV 05 I've never learned the story of St Sebastian. I flip through my art books and see various perspectives on the day he was executed. Sometimes I truly relate to the paintings on the canvas. Bound and tied to a tree to be shot with arrows. I am under investigation yet again. This is becoming a by-monthly event. Every instance involves me using a little thing I like to call common sense. I'm 24 and have about 1½ years of combat experience I am responsible for 5 men. We are tight net and with out question have always accomplished the mission. I have been "weathered." Now you take our LT. He is 24 and is responsible for 20 men. He has 4 months of combat experience and has never been "in contact. Only in the

St Sebastian

97

18 Nov

I've been in several mosques for different reasons both overseas and in the states. They are usually very simple structures with an open room. No pews, no entertainment centers. Only a window or sometimes a place where glass should be that faces Mecca depending on where you are in the world. The congregation discusses blessings and events on the lawn that usually surrounds the building. I'm not saying their way is the right way, but imagine a simple faith, one where faith was the reason for going. I still very much enjoy the goings on of our faith's community. I just think we could learn a lot from each other. Right now we are at FOB Gecko. My men just brought me food. Variety is not something we enjoy here. [It's the] same food no matter where you go, and all of it sucks. Oh well, it could be worse.

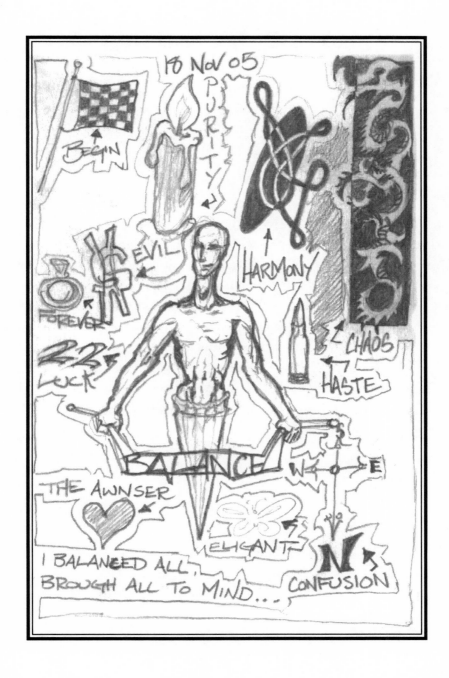

2 Dec 05

Spending most of my nights walking up mountains, most of my dawns looking down the back side of those mountains, and most of my days running down bad guys on motorcycles. "Win hearts and minds." The last war we committed ourselves to that tactic was Vietnam. Long, painful, and we still lost. I am losing patience and belief in the cause every day. I threw a man last night. There was cause for it—lack of time and incoming mortar rounds. I still almost feel bad for doing it. The peanut stuff you sent has been so good. There are twenty-one of us here and we all appreciate it very much. I need to get some sleep. The sun is getting ready to set, and I haven't rested in a few days. Good night.

3 Dec 05

I'm sick, tired, and useless. I haven't been able to keep anything in my stomach for the last couple days. We're staying in a mud hut we acquired from this guy and his wife. When we leave, his whole family will probably be killed for involuntarily aiding American soldiers. I cannot put into words how much I hate the United States government. It eats me alive when I think about the needless BS they put us through. No one knows what's going on and no one really cares, with the exception of the families of loved ones back in the States. I am at the end of my rope.

I try to think about home. I try to remember the details that never change. I'm so depressed and defeated right now. I am too weak to go out with my men. I will never forgive myself if something happens to them. I wish I had the stones to just say no. No, I will not pick up another rifle. No, I will not kill another man. I hate myself in times like this. Thinking about the things I've done. I fear I will never forgive myself. I just feel like I've been driven down to my knees. I'll push on to tomorrow in the pace. It's all we have sometimes: tomorrow.

10 Dec 05

Where to begin? Well, I guess where I left off. I have recovered from my illness. B., the Lt., and D. air force controller ran over an IED. First Scouts to get severely wounded here. Lt. F. and D. received burns and B. lost a leg. They should all recover. When the blast went off, me, SSG Stockard, Drake, and Shank got on dirt bikes to run a TACSAT radio down to the site to order a dust off (MEDEVAC helicopter). While we were moving, the call was made on a Thuraya satellite phone. We linked up with TM3 three kilometers from the blast site. One truck was destroyed, two were stuck, and one was the only mobile vehicle.

The first night was getting trucks unstuck and no sleep. Since we rolled out on dirt bikes we took fire moving to the blast site. I was ahead, so I didn't take any fire. The other guys got pinned down for a few minutes until the ANA was able to suppress the enemy with machine guns and RPGs.

The other night we received the first food in three days. We had just settled down to eat when a round impacted about thirty feet away. RPGs throw a lot of dirt in the air but they have to be pretty close to do real damage. Some guys got pinned down in a compound at the base of the hill I was on. With about eight other Scouts we laid down some crazy lead. We didn't kill any enemy to our knowledge. We took fire from a hill.

Over five days we were in contact with the enemy for four of those days. No food, little sleep. They took the trucks out and we walked back. I forgot to mention twenty-eight dudes from Battle Co. came out to support us; they ate our remaining food. Water wasn't an issue because we had a river nearby. Walking up and down mountains, running through the river. Freezing temperatures (the low was 29 degrees).

Then, they told us we had to move by foot at night back to our safety house. Guess who was on point? Yup, yours truly. Moved in line on an IED-infested road at night. We made it back with only two cold-weather injuries. We could have been helo'd out, but a long story short, we weren't and now we may have to walk fifteen kilometers to Balo, the closest FOB nearby. This is hands down the most draining experience I have ever had. Lord, give us strength. This, too, shall pass.

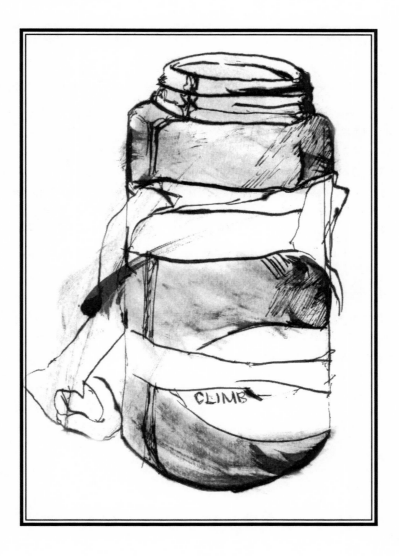

I'm ready to break. I push my tolerance further back with each shot fired, every meal missed, and every step in the darkness. The cold pierces my soul. My body shuts down one piece at a time. Reality slips in the process. At night, moving in the cold and pain of hunger, I can see little demon-like creatures. Their eyes flash red as they scurry around and sit on rocks as I pass. The imagination is contorted in pain. I am ready to be finished. Don't let me break.

This too shall pass; I can't find a reason to justify my ways. I don't want to hear the lies of the puppet masters to make me feel better.

As I sit here and slowly close my eyes, I ease my soul by telling myself I need to seek the serenity in providing a shield for an ignorant people from an evil that could be compared to the power and illusiveness of a dragon. Will I ever know the freedom I tell myself we provide? When will I stop? When is the cold of winter going to take the fight out of what enemy is left? I could really use a pause to reality.

I'M READY TO BREAK
I PUSH MY TOLERANCE
FURTHER BACK WITH
EACH SHOT FIRED
EVERY MEAL MISSED
AND EVERY STEP IN
THE DARKNESS. THE
COLD PIERESS MY
SOUL MY BODY
SHUTS DOWN ONE
PIECE AT A TIME.
REALITY SLIPS IN
THE PROCESS.
AT NIGHT MOVING
IN THE COLD
AND PAIN OF
HUNGER I CAN
SEE LITTLE DEMON
LIKE CREATURES,
THEIR EYES FLASH
RED AS THEY
SCURRY AROUND
AND SIT ON ROCKS
AS I PASS. THE
IMAGINATION IS
CONTORTED IN
PAIN. I AM READY
FOR THIS TO BE
FINISHED. DON'T
LET ME BREAK.

THIS
TO
SHALL
PASS

I CAN'T FIND
A REASON TO
JUSTIFY MY
WAYS. I DON'T
WANT TO HEAR
THE LIES OF
THE PUPPET
MASTERS TO
MAKE ME
FEEL BETTER

AS I SIT HERE
AND SLOWLY
CLOSE MY EYES. I
EASE MY SOUL BY
TELLING MY SELF
I NEED TO SEEK
THE SERENITY
IN PROVIDING
A SHIELD FOR
AN IGNORANT
PEOPLE FROM
AN EVIL THAT
COULD BE
COMPARED TO
THE POWER AND
ILLUSIVENESS OF
A DRAGON. WILL
I EVER KNOW THE
FREEDOM I TELL
MYSELF WE
PROVIDE. WHEN
WILL I STOP
WHEN IS THE
COLD OF WINTER
GOING TO TAKE
THE FIGHT OUT
OF WHAT ENEM
IS LEFT. I
COULD REALLY
USE A PAUSE
TO REALITY.

11 Dec 05

I didn't tell Aaron [little brother] happy birthday. I don't know why, but that hurts so bad I feel like crying. Have I been a good brother and son? I've always run. Run from love, problems, and relationships. I don't run anymore. I remember when Aaron locked himself in the elevator at Grandma's wedding. I feel that same terror when one of my guys gets pinned down and I can't help. When I almost broke his foot at Mom's wedding. I feel the same guilt when I killed that kid in Iraq. When he tells me about his truck and his work, I feel the same pride when my men get kudos from an unexpected source. God knows I love him. The times I left him behind because I told him he was too small. I know he will succeed at whatever he does. He has a heart of gold and a drive that cannot be compared to anything on this earth. I'm so proud of him. Time for sleep. Happy late birthday, little brother. Keep your eyes up, your heart pure, and your path righteous. Never forget I love you and am always with you. Happy birthday again from your brother, W.

Andar, Afghanistan, Keybay Valley

11 DEC 05

I DIDN'T TELL AARON HAPPY BIRTHDAY.
I DON'T KNOW WHY BUT THAT HURTS SO BAD
I FEEL LIKE CRYING. HAVE I BEEN A GOOD
BROTHER AND SON. I'VE ALWAYS RAN. RAN
FROM LOVE, PROBLEMS AND RELATIONSHIPS.
I DON'T RUN ANY MORE. I REMEMBER WHEN
AARON LOCKED HIMSELF IN THE ELEVATOR
AT GRANDMA'S WEDDING. I FEEL THAT SAME
TERROR WHEN ONE OF MY GUYS GETS PINNED
DOWN AND I CAN'T HELP. WHEN I ALMOST
BROKE HIS FOOT AT MOM'S WEDDING. I FEEL
THE SAME GUILT WHEN I KILLED THAT KID
IN IRAQ. WHEN HE TELLS ME ABOUT HIS
TRUCK AND HIS WORK I FEEL THE SAME
PRIDE WHEN MY MEN GET KUDO'S FROM
AN UNEXPECTED SOURCE. GOD KNOWS I
LOVE HIM. THE TIMES I LEFT HIM BEHIND
BECAUSE I TOLD HIM HE WAS TO SMALL I
KNOW HE WILL SUCEED AT WHAT EVER HE
DOES HE HAS A HEART OF GOLD AND A
DRIVE THAT CANNOT BE COMPARED TO ANYTHING
ON THIS EARTH. I'M SO PROUD OF HIM.
TIME FOR SLEEP. HAPPY LATE BIRTHDAY
LITTLE BROTHER. KEEP YOUR EYES UP,
YOUR HEART PURE, AND YOUR PATH
RIGHTEOUS. NEVER FORGET I LOVE YOU AND
AM ALWAYS WITH YOU. HAPPY BIRTHDAY
AGIAN FROM YOUR BRO. W ANDAR, AFGHANISTAN
                        KEYBAY VALLEY

12 Dec 05

The balance of life. Can you have good without evil? Do the bad things exist because, if they didn't, eventually something would break down? It's hard to imagine, even harder to explain. We are what we need to be when the time calls for it. Seeing us now playing cards and relaxing, you couldn't picture us killing the enemy just a few days ago. We are a strange form of balance. One extreme to the other with little transition. We should be back on the 14th; we'll see.

The balance of
life. Can you have
good without evil?
Do the bad things
exist because if
they didn't even-
tually something
would break
down. It's hard
to imagine even
harder to explain.
We are what we
need to be when
the time calls
for it. Seeing
us now playing
cards and relaxing
you couldn't picture
us killing the
enemy just a few
days ago. We are
a strange form
of balance. One
extreme to the
other with little
transition. We
should be back on
the 14TH, we'll see.

WAR

HATE

BROKEN

LOST

EMPTY

DESTRUCTION

CONFUSION

PEACE

LOVE

BALANCE

FAITH

ENLIGHTEN
MENT

ENJOYMENT

EQUALITY

13 Dec 05

Question is, what have you accomplished here? The person I am asking can interpret it however he wants, and I will edit the answers so they are mom-appropriate.

- S. - Sniper - Gave people a change (Afghan people).
- Sh. — JTAC - Here as in earth … I've learned.
- P. - ATL/Aspiring Congressman - How to use the slit trench without pissing on my leg.
- Sprague - Senior Scout Observer/Spotter - Nothing.
- Drake - Sniper - Unwanted and unnecessary abuse of my body.
- Linville - RTO - Never start outside of the circle.
- WOJO - Sniper - Be careful what you wish for.
- Lt. M .- FSO - Boxing.
- R. - LLVI - I can't think of nothing.
- A. - TL - There's a surprise behind every corner.
- R. - Interpreter - I can't say shit.
- S. - SQD LDR - All of this we've done won't mean shit in fifty years.
- L. - Medic - Almost finished my time in the army.

So that's the average idea among those stranded in Andar today. I guess my answer would be, not enough. So the day goes on. We are all just wasting time. Tomorrow night we are supposed to get extracted back to Lagham. We'll see if that happens. We are wearing down. Tempers get short in times like these. Patience—[that's] the only thing we really have control over here and how I've handled things.

13 Dec 05

We're sitting around a fire telling ghost stories, and I think Aunt Judy saved my life. I wrote you how that guy had the drop on me in the Arghandab Valley. That shine caught my eye and gave away the position of the guy swinging the rifle on me. When me and Dad got into it or I would have a problem, I would go to Aunt Judy's house, smoke cigarettes on her porch, and figure things out. When I enlisted, Aunt Judy would tell me when I got scared or had a problem not to worry because she would be my light. That's all she would say is that she would be my light. Aunt Judy died two days before that day in the valley. That shine saved my life. I think Aunt Judy had a lot to do with it. Just writing her name hurts my heart. She was such an awesome person. I need to pay my respects when I get home.

3 Jan 06

"Primum est non nocere"

First, do no harm; Latin. The holiday season is a depressing time here. It's been just over a week since Christmas. Feels like a month. Time is dragging by so slow. Being stagnant drives me up the walls. We are so much closer to leaving, but ten months have worn me down. We are all drawing from patience we don't know. We have to stay somewhat polite with our company. The temp has dropped. With the exception of a few two or three day missions, I know we will be here watching the days roll by one after another until we leave this place and return. Return. What a concept. I have never felt fear in the moment of a fight or a battle. The fear is most intense in the anticipation leading up to the events. I fear going home. I fear how I will be perceived by those I love. I fear what me and my girlfriend have. I have always been a runner. I am always moving. I am a refugee from all things solid. So lost. I usually prefer to be alone. I find a familiar comfort in new friends. Once again, loathing in the winter of my discontent. I guess all things change. I imagine I probably need to change with them. I need to figure out so much. Seven years of this. The sad thing is I'm not sure what I've even accomplished; I'm twenty-five. Need to clear my head of too many pieces that don't fit.

The holidays are always a hard time in the army. Even if you're home, the thought of not being back for the following year is always in the back of your mind. That's the reason I think I haven't written anything for a while. I think about mountains and meadows, forests with huge green valleys, and cool ponds and streams to swim and fish in. I remember my first time in the Arabah Valley and the first time I [reached the] summit in the Alps of Mont Blanc. Seeing that much beauty made my heart hurt. The time I swam in the creek in Hatcher Pass. I kept my eyes at water level as this beaver swam ten feet from my face. I remember the first time I kissed my girlfriend. How much pain was in my chest. My heart broke because I was leaving her in a week to return to prepare to leave for war. So many things I have to be grateful for seeing. So many experiences. The night Chemical Ali was taken down and we moved into one of his palaces in Iraq, the people had parades in the streets. Memorials were built for the people he had tortured. So much history. I was in Kirkuk when Baghdad fell, in Fallujah when Uday and Qusay were killed. I saw the hole Saddam was found in. The last years of my life have revolved around some form of death. I will be happy to turn in my ammo for the last time, to lock my rifle up in a cage and never have to touch it again. I just pray it treats the next owner as good as it did me. I pray so much; I wonder if I will go to heaven. I am at peace with the things I've done. I just don't know if I can be forgiven.

Unity of my team, recon symbol/H7K Triangle Spearhead – one-team two – brothers I've lost, men I've killed – Tip of the spear recon triangle

The tattoo I gave myself Christmas night and into the hours of my birthday. The present I gave myself. Not many people can say they gave themselves a tattoo, fewer still in Afghanistan. It's meaningful to me in so many ways. As are my other two. The cross on my arm is so I always have family with me. The hawk on my leg is in memory of a good friend who believed that when he died a hawk would take him to his fathers. Time for sleep. Good night, Mom.

6 Jan 05

I have been on point in jungles, through forests, mountain ranges, deserts, and the artic. Right now I feel like I've felt when I've realized I don't have a clue where I am.

Panic sets in and you don't know which way is up. In Thailand I was on point for a twenty-click movement (about twelve miles). Fourteen clicks into it, we came under triple canopy so dark our night vision wouldn't even work. That's when the "uchowees" come out. All you hear throughout the trees is, "Hey, where the fuck are we?" That's how I feel right now, like one of the guys in the back without a map. I know I'll get through it. There's only been one time where I didn't get us to the objective on time, but that involved a huge moose with a very short temper. We got there only four or five minutes late. Dad, I actually had a conversation with him, like a talk, you know. He also sent me my first letter the other day. The world never stops surprising me. Oh well, what am I going do with my life? Team 3 got hit tonight. Contrary to popular belief, I think we are going to have to fight to our last days here.

RAGE
FRUSTRITON
FURY

18 Jan 06

The weather is changing. There's a warm front coming through and low-level clouds billowing over the mountains. The barometer is jumping around like a two-year-old [child]. We're in for a storm. The weather report isn't calling for snow, but I think it's getting ready to dump on us. I've felt electricity in the air like this before in Alaska; it's coming. It's getting closer, us going back. One day at a time. I'm still not sleeping, but now it's not for the bad dreams; it's more anxiety. I'm going to Scott's wedding in Colorado. Driving around to visit friends both dead and alive. I think seeing headstones is going to be something I am definitely going to do. There's just so much I'm going to do. Doing whatever I want—what a concept. The freedom we paid for, for so long.

I hold onto pain like it's a thing of value.

- It becomes a part of me like marrow or sinew.
- I treasure it because I'm lost.
- I keep it close as I ignore the cost.
- I hope soon I can release.
- I hope one day I will find comfort with my hands in prayer on my knees.
- I ask forgiveness but I never let go.
- Why do I tax my spirit this way? I hope from it I can one day grow.
- When this is finished I know I'll be stronger.
- When I let go from a point that can haunt me no longer.

In life, one of the things I've learned but have never applied is if I want balance and true happiness, I need to let go. I will.

FURIOUS ANGEL

16 Jan 06

Yesterday—I was supposed to be out of the army yesterday. I should be home today. All this should have been over for me; it's not. We are still very much in this. There are only a few pages in your book. Only two months left here. Two months. People say how fast time has gone by. I've never heard that here. Very rarely do we bring up how much time we have left. So much can happen in a minute around here, let alone a day or a week. Time has never gone by fast, not here. Time won't even pick up for me in firefights anymore. Days just kind of float around and linger like clouds. When you don't pay attention, they change. Eleven new guys are coming in tomorrow. Me and my snipers are going to make sure they can shoot. First, we'll make sure their weapons are zeroed, then we will see if they can shoot under stress.

25 Jan 06

I sit quietly in my thoughts as the night passes. Thinking of sleep. Dreaming of a life that I pray one day I will get to live. Tomorrow is another day. Another mission. Another hunt. There was a time when I enjoyed this life. When the thought of the fight was all I could think about. The idea that I was making a difference. Now the thought of battle brings fear of death and memories of loss. Nothing in me is the same. Every belief, moral, and concept is changed. With the ones I love I try to present myself in a way that is good. One day I hope to be normal again. Not for a while. Not until I detach myself from this way of life. I need sleep. Good night, Mom.

2 Feb 06

Well, here I am. We have just established Wildcat Base. We are inside the village of Mizan right next to Arghandab Valley. I pray we never have to drive through there. I hate that place. This compound we are in now isn't that bad, besides the fact they dumped wheat all over the floor, it got wet, fermented, and is producing ammonia. [It's a] bleed-from-your-eyes type of atmosphere. Besides that, it really isn't that bad here. I still don't know what happened with my girlfriend. We broke up about a week ago. I don't know why. She was pretty mean to me, she dumped me, then she hung up. I think everything just kind of got to her at once. Then she took it out on me, which is OK. What wasn't cool was when she hung up on me. I don't play bullshit high school games anymore. My men are a great group of guys. They heard about some military intelligence girl who has a crush on me, they got me an "appointment" to "debrief" her on a few sectors, and, yeah, so basically it's as close to a date as I am going to get. I guess there is no way to get over the last one like the next one. That and I enjoy breaking rules. I haven't even had a conversation with a woman in person since I was home. I am not over my girlfriend. I just can't let it get to me. I'll be OK. I always am.

4 Feb 06

This place isn't that bad. One of the best places I've stayed outside of Lagham. We did village assessments today. This whole district is held together by a hot spring that pumps fresh water. Crazy to see people as dependent on nature as these people are. There isn't another water source for twenty miles. If I had to live in this country, I would probably stay somewhere around here. Between the Kerosene lantern, the diesel-burning heater, and the ammonia-sweating floor, we are all developing a chest pain and a cough. I'd rather feel like crap than be cold. Fifty days left, plus or minus. Time should really start to slow down now.

7 Feb 06

We were informed today that we are to move our gear into the transient tents when we get back to Lagham, or we have until the twenty-eighth to have it done anyway. We are all packed up and ready to hit the highway. Been ready. We are a little over a month out and they still don't have a clue. I try not to care but I do. Last night some asshole blew himself up putting a bomb in the road. Better him than us. When Muslims greet each other, they say, "Salam alaykum," which means "Peace be with you." The thing is I have only met a few who know the concept of the word peace. Every once in a while I will run into guys I haven't seen in a while. These people can't sit still. They just can't. They're going to get us in a fight. These bastards [are] constantly going. All they want is to fight. I fear they'll get it.

SCARS OF BATTLE

Scars of battle are not only held in flesh and skin; those are normally the only ones noticed. Some scars run so deep the only place they can be seen is through the eyes. Flesh wounds heal. Bones mend and skin regenerates. The heart goes numb, the soul grows cold, and the conscience is silenced. Those are the ones that keep me awake at night. They get me out of bed and have me walk a perimeter even if one doesn't exist. So many memories, too many faces. In the night staring at the ceiling I can see [some] of the faces of men whom I have killed. Sometimes it's like counting sheep or looking at stuffed animals. Other times it's a confrontation that will not let me rest. I have to walk up the side of a mountain in a few hours, but I can't sleep. I can hear voices and shouting. Sometimes even a full-on firefight. The thing that really kills me is I can't turn away from it. I can't leave it alone. It's like I need it. There isn't much more to killing a man than pulling a trigger or applying the use of a knife. The necessity of that life is what breaks me down. The less I try to think about it, the more it haunts me. The more I think about it, the colder I become. I've tried to give it to God, but I am tired of patience. I know there's a God. I am sorry. So sorry for what I've done. I just wish He would let up on me sometimes. I don't know what plans He has for me but I hope they are pretty damn important for all the pain I endure.

Boondock Saints

Never shall innocent blood be shed. Yet the blood of the wicked shall flow like a river. We three shall spread our blackened wings and be the vengeful striking hammer of God. You people have been chosen to reveal our existence to the world. You will witness what happens here today and you will tell of it later. All eyes to the front. Now you will receive us. We do not ask for your poor or your hungry. We do not want your tired and sick. It is your corrupt we claim. It is your evil that will be sought by us. With every breath we shall hunt them down. Each day we will spill their blood 'till it rains down from the skies. Do not kill, do not rape, do not steal. These are principles that every man of every faith can embrace. These are not polite suggestions; these are codes of behavior and those of you who ignore them will pay the dearest cost. There are varying degrees of evil. We allowed you lesser forms of filth not to push the bounds and cross over into true corruption, into our domain. For if you do, one day you will look behind you and you will see we three, and on that day you will reap it. And we will send you to whatever god you wish. And shepherds we shall be for thee, my Lord, for thee. Thou hath descended forth through thine hand. I will swiftly carry out thy command. So we shall hold the river forth to thee and, teeming with souls, shall it ever be.

Nomine Patris, et Filii, et Spiritus Sancti

BALANCE IN CHAOS,
CAN ONE EXSIST IN
THE FULL PRESS
OF THE OTHER?
CAN THEY FUNCTION
IN THE SAME
ENVIORMENT?
I TRY TO
TAKE
THE
GOOD
WITH
THE
BAD
AND
THE
LOVE
WITH
THE
HATE
IT
JUST
SEEMS
LIKE
REGARDLESS
OF HOW
HARD YOU TRY
PEACE CAN
ONLY BE
FOUND IN
SMALL
MOMENTS
THAT
PASS
LIKE
THE CALM
BEFORE
A STORM.
IN THIS
PLACE IT'S
VERY RARE
THAT I GO TO
BED NOT FEELING
DEFEATED EVEN THOUGH
WE TOOK THE VICTORY.

15 Feb 06

We are out in Mizan hunting for Taliban. We have been observed by at least two of their scouts. They know who we are from the H&K insignia on our trucks. We listen to their conversations on the radio. We have an idea of who they are, Pakistani from their dialect. We think. Someone brought up how much time we have left in the country; we have a "source" in headquarters. He manifested our names for the 21 of March. It looks like I might make it back in time to tell you happy birthday from Italy or Kandahar at the least. Thirty-two days and a wake-up. God keep us. Bring my men home safe.

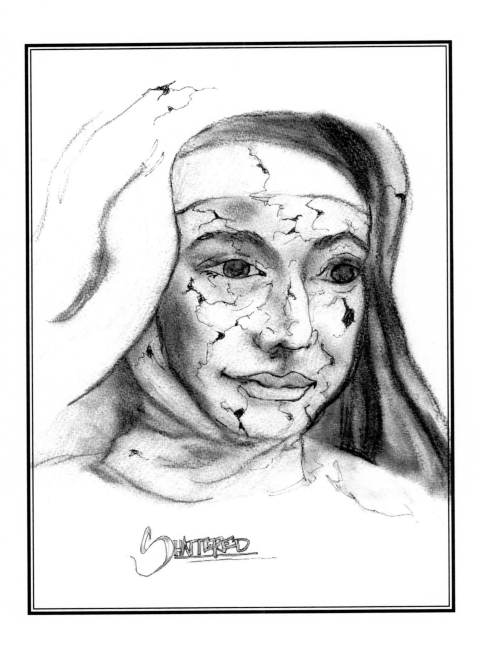

17 Feb 06

The rain is falling. The air smells fresh. I'm out on a small cement porch listening to old, old music. The music that kind of grabs you. Nina Simone and Billie Holiday. Slow and aggressive at the same time. I like music that speaks to me. We walked through a valley that runs east out of Mizan today. The walls of granite were screaming to be climbed as I watched their crests for movement as we walked the floor. A small creek carved its way through the gravel bedrock. We continue to look for the enemy. Spring is here, and the Taliban are trafficking weapons and munitions. Two guys from B Company were MEDEVACed yesterday. They got hit just outside of Andar. I wrote about that place. I remember daily attacks and running out of food. I need to get my men out of here safe. If one of them gets hurt, it will destroy me.

20 Feb 06

I am at my breaking point. The only thing I care about is getting my men home safe. We have a short, angry man who is responsible for the battalion's ops. His tunnel vision doesn't exceed his military progress. He is so fixated on what he wants done, he exploits whomever he has to. I have held the flag as eighteen coffins have been carried onto planes to be sent back to their families. I have never seen him at any of those ceremonies. The thing that gets me even more is that his decisions played a major part in their deaths. I am losing all respect for the Afghani people. They don't care if we're here. I talked to a farmer today who said, "Americans are going to fight someone no matter what. Why should I care if you die? It doesn't affect me either way."

Lord, I am falling apart. I am torn mentally, physically, emotionally, and spiritually. I am losing the path. Lord, give me focus. Give me rest. My men, my leaders, their families, and my own are depending on me. All this weight is running me into the ground. I don't know what I need. I am so lost right now. My hope is fading. I will try harder, Lord, but I need guidance. I need a direction. You know I will stay on point regardless of the situation. I am just so very hateful right now I can't think. Give me a direction, Lord. Keep my men safe, Father. Forgive me for my sins. Thank you for today and help me through tomorrow. Amen.

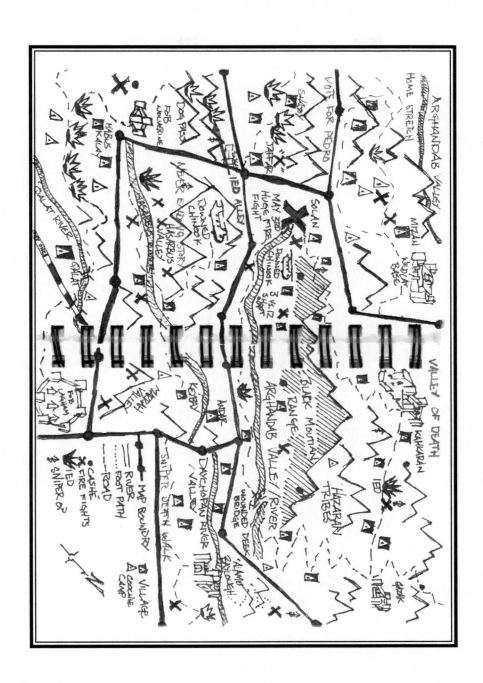

20 Feb 06 1930Z 2400 Local

It's midnight, and we are waiting for an attack. We have men manning the towers and mortars and listening to radios. No rest yet again. This is how this place gets you. When you are down, something like this happens and just tacks the nails in for you. "Inevitable attack" right ... They are collecting bits and pieces of intel over a CB radio. God I need some DAMNED SLEEP, DO YOU HEAR ME!!!!?!! No, I guess not. It looks like I might be walking up a fucking mountain instead.

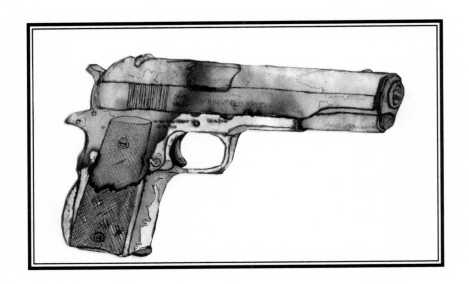

22 Feb 06

Two is my lucky number. I don't think you know that. Here are some coincidences that led me to that. In Airborne School, my roster number was 222. When I went to Alaska, I was a machine gunman; my gun was #2. When I was an RTO, my radio's serial number was 02202. In Italy I live on 220 Donizziti on the second floor. When I was in Iraq, my call sign was Chosen 2 Bravo. Bravo being the letter "B," which is the second letter in the alphabet. Here, my call sign is Wildcat 2 Alpha. I am on Team 2, and this is my second deployment working for Shane, whose first name is also William. My favorite sister was born on the twenty-second, as was my favorite mom. So, I guess the number two was good luck before I was even born. Whenever I see the number two I know I will be OK. Strange.

Before I got this book I was in a pretty vicious fight in Shindkay, just south of Sweeney. I killed three men that day. One of them about hit me. Wasn't my day. We moved down the valley to clean the bodies. We got some of their scouts. It was kind of spooky, killing enemy counterparts. They traveled like us, light on motorcycles. They had more "boom" than chow and water. So many similarities. I killed the Afghan version of me that day. There were a lot of rounds exchanged. How we all got out of that one without any casualties still gets me thinking sometimes. I remember feeling a really intense form of guilt when I saw these dead fish I had killed when I launched grenades at one of the fighters. It really bothered me. It still does when I think about it. We saved lives that day, no question. That was an intense fight. Those guys were warriors. I respect them. I shot one of them in the shoulder and spun him around; he still got back up and returned fire so his buddy could move to get behind cover. Thinking about that kind of valor almost makes me choke up. Almost. According to our new schedule we have twenty days and a wake-up. That's it, one month. One cycle of the moon, two paychecks and we are done. I have a desperate anxiety to eat good food and drink wine. I'm nervous about seeing the family, seeing old friends. I know it's silly, but I feel like I'll never fit in again. I've been on the outside looking in for so long. I'll be OK. I'll figure it out when the time comes. I've always been a good planner but a better improviser. I'm going to ride for a while.

23 Feb 06

This morning we were going out on a foot recon. When we passed through Mizan some jerk almost ran one of my men over. Gave Vinne a pretty good scare. When I confronted the guy, he started laughing. I snapped. I beat the smile off his face. I would have killed him had Shane not thrown me on the ground. Our cops got in a firefight later this afternoon. The popular belief is we are out-numbered. The Taliban are gathering in villages to mass an attack. First light we go hunting. This was not the news we wanted to hear. No holds barred. Tomorrow is going to be a bad day. I wonder how many more men will die before I go home. Father, forgive me. Bring my men home safe before myself.

25 Feb 06

We have been in and out of contact the last couple of days. Tomorrow we are staging for an attack the following day. This place. We are taking our gun trucks on this one. Lord, have mercy on the souls of those we send to meet St. Peter. Not a good day to be Taliban. We're staging weapons hot for our remaining time here. No more games. We will be out here until the third now. We were supposed to be finished with combat ops a month ago. I can't wait to work for men who don't spend 80 percent of their time on their knees making other men happy. Lord, forgive me of my sins and bring my men home safely. Let us go without a firefight this month.

Before the "Army of One"
Before the "Kinder, Gentler Army"
There were the "Grunts"

27 Feb 06

We went out the last two days and tried to pick a fight. The Taliban didn't so much as make a sound. They stayed off their radios and out of sight. It was nice. Some guys from 20 Mountain 4-22nd infantry met us out there. Those guys were as green as the grass. They were afraid of their own shadows. They asked us why we sleep in our HWMM-Vs so we start rambling off stories of ambushes and mortar attacks. They are in for a long year. I made a comment in front of the wrong person; I will be visiting a shrink before we get back to Italy. So we'll see how that goes. The powers that be are saying all the scouts will be seeing a head doctor because, "You recon guys have been through too much not to have PTSD." I just wanted to say thanks for putting us through all that. Lord, thank you for today, and help me get through tomorrow.

27–28 Feb, Midnight 2 Time:

Last day of the month is winding out. I have fifteen minutes left on my guard shift. Times like these are lonely ones, but I enjoy the quiet on radio guard. It gives me time to let my brain just kind of unwind and go neutral for a while; that's a very rare event here. Twenty-three days and a wake-up.

We are possibly turning our trucks over to 10th Mountain on the 7th. I hope that comes through. If it does, that means no more ops for my guys. I will still have to go out on RIPs (relief in place) to be a backseat driver, but my guys will get to rest. Thank you, Lord, for today; bring my men home safe and help me through tomorrow.

1 March 06

So I have news. I am living in Candy Land now. Two reasons behind that. The first is scouts need a liaison to help push out our equipment. The second is because Shane has been keeping an eye on me, and he says I never sleep. I told him I do, just not that much. Long story short, I am seeing doctors for my "sleeping disorder," PTSD, and "aggressive behavior directed toward Afghan nationals." They gave me my own room with a shower down the hall and an Internet connection gets put in tomorrow. Not a bad gig. Doc gave me sleeping pills today; I can't wait to sleep.

2 March:

Yeah, that sleeping pill really worked. I slept a whole night for the first time in months. Felt so good to wake up with the sun coming through the window. Tomorrow I go to see Doc again. He's a good guy. I like him because he tells me he knows he won't understand all the things in my head, but he wants to help me sort them out and deal with my problems. I respect that. My pill is kicking in. I can feel the sleep coming. Usually I have to wait for sleep, but now it comes for me. Good night, Mom. I'm getting better, step by step.

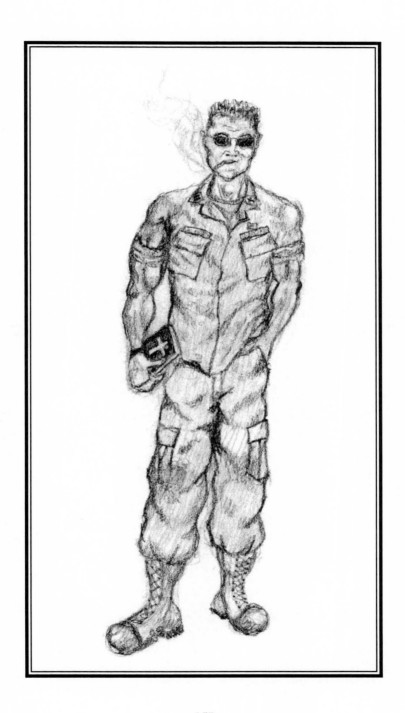

14 March 06

Seven days left. One week. I have seen the last full moon I am going to see in this country. I am ready to get back. We will probably have to stay two or three days in Manas, Tajikistan.

I don't know if the army is going to provide medical benefits for me when I get out. To be honest, if they are going to make this a long battle, I will just get out without. The army has already drained me so much. I really don't feel like fighting for this. I will be good regardless. The stress is already coming down quite a bit just being this close. I am going to put this book away so I can write in Italy.

12 Apr 06

It's over. I am home. Scott is living with me. Everything is so amazing for me right now. I have been sleeping and climbing. People are in and out of my house all the time, so I am never alone. Mom, I feel so good. There is nothing I have planned in the future that involves a weapon or violence. Just logistical ends to tie up and I will be home. Thank God.

19 April 06

Right now I am waiting at the train station. I came a couple hours early so I could walk around before they showed. The weather is perfect. The cherry blossoms are floating around. Kind of peaceful. Actually, very peaceful. I enjoy hearing the birds, distant conversations, and kids laughing as they play. I am so at ease right now. I signed out on leave; no work for twenty-five days. So awesome. I am unwinding in a way I haven't since I found out I was going to Iraq. Just peace. I feel so good. Life is good. I will see you soon. All my love. —W.

29 April 06

On a train bound for Rome. It's quiet. The trains have this way of putting me to sleep. Life is good. Traveling is good; it brings adventure. I like adventure. I will draw you a picture in Rome so I will save some space here.

5 May:

I was going to draw something, but I am leaving Sicily to go to Naples. I promise I will draw you something. I just don't know when. I am doing very well just enjoying everything and meeting awesome people. I love you and will call you tonight.

18 June 06

On the train [coming] back from Rome. I love that place, staying in hostels, and just enjoying life. Yet again, the French set the example of why I don't like them. They think I can't understand what they are saying. I am myself again. I will be home so very soon. Cannot wait.

18 June 06.—On the train back from Rome. I love that place staying in hostels and just enjoying life. Yet again the French set the example of why I don't like them. They th I can't understand what they are saying. I am myself again. I will be home so very soon. Can not wait.

June 2, 5:42 AM

I just pulled over right on the Arizona side of the mountains before Yuma to see the sun come up. Never seen a more perfect sunrise. I wonder if it was intended for me. It's over. Finally finished. I finish this chapter of my life now. I think the perfect sunrise and waking my mom up in person for the first time in too long is the perfect way to start a new life. I love you, Mom.

MY MOTHER'S
LOVE

IT MAKES ME WARM
ON FRIGID NIGHTS
IT GIVES ME STRENGTH
WHEN I CAN'T GO ON
IT COMFORTS ME WHEN
NO ONE CAN

IT IS ALWAYS WITH ME
AND NEVER FAILING
IT TAUGHT ME RIGHT FROM
WRONG
IT SHOWED ME PATIENCE
THE VIRTUE
IT GOT ME THROUGH THE HARD
TIMES WHEN THE HARD
TIMES GOT THROUGH ME

IT REACHED FOR ME AS I
RAN AWAY
IT EMBRACED ME AS I
FELL
IT WELCOMED ME AS
I APROACHED

IT HAS BEEN WITH ME THROUGH IT ALL, THE SLIPS
THE FALLS, THE COLD, THE MUDD, THE SNOW, THE RAIN,
THE PAIN, THE HEARTACHES, THE DECISIONS, THE
TROUBLE. NEAR OR FAR IT'S ALWAYS WITH ME IT
HAS AND WILL STICK THROUGH THIS LIFE AND
THERE AFTER.

TO ALL THE WOMEN WHO HAVE BEEN MOTHERS TO
ME I WILL NEVER FORGET, EVER
— Will

Places to go

- Mount Sinai at dawn
- Eliat, Israel's most southern city
- Jerusalem Holy Tour, Villa De La Rosa, Jesus's trail with the cross
- Cairo, pyramids
- Auschwitz, Poland
- Valley East of Mizan Two Shiny Nickels—NO NEVER AGAIN
- Dublin (Blarney Stone)
- Austria, Auschwitz
- Germany, Berlin, Black Forest
- Normandy, D Day, Omaha Beach
- Holland, Amsterdam
- Switzerland, Andermatt and Zurich
- Zimbabwe
- Romania, Transylvania
- Estonia
- Kyrgyzstan
- Prague
- Australia, New South Wales
- Tasmania
- Thailand
- Budapest, Hungary

My Friends
15 Fallen Brothers
Never Forget

11 WIA Purple Hearts

Cops killed Afghan - 33 hash marks
Cops wounded Afghan – 23 hash marks

AFTERWORDS

Through the eyes of Lauren Hughes

AFTER COMBAT AND RETURNING back to the states, Will struggled internally for many years. Returning back to civilization was hell for him mostly because the grace period was over for not having to think and process all that he had just done, witnessed, and been a part of. Being in combat doesn't give you much time to grieve your brother that was just killed, to think of the decision you just made, to process the fact of how close to death you had just come, or to think about why you survived while others did not. The responsibility he felt for the survival and safety of his men along with the adrenaline and chaos of war was what made it possible for him to push it down as best he could in the moment and move on to do whatever needed to be done next.

Once Will was no longer in combat there was too much time to think and having time to think is quite often never good for a combat veteran. Will couldn't stop the nightmares. He couldn't stop the fear that he now had the time to truly feel. He couldn't stop the immense grief or the anger or the guilt any more than he could stop the constant ringing in his ears or the pain and discomfort from all the injuries he had suffered while in combat. The broken bones that, like his mind during war, were never given the time they needed to properly heal, caused him constant pain. Survival mode had become his life. It was the only way he knew how to survive and live.

What used to be the simplest parts of life were no longer simple. Even down to what to sleep in at night in order to feel safe. In combat, often times the night is the most terrifying and dangerous time. It is usually when soldiers are the most afraid because they are unable to see what is coming. During combat most soldiers are too alert to sleep and so they drift in and out of half consciousness, always listening for approaching danger. They have their gear on and their gun close, ready to engage at any moment. When they return to society the fear and nightmares keep most soldiers from ever sleeping in peace again. Living in combat causes soldiers to constantly be on alert at all times. Will was also no longer able to simply go into a restaurant and enjoy a good meal. Instead, from the moment he entered the room he would have an escape plan. He always knew where he would go for cover if someone started shooting in that moment. He would constantly be scanning the room, every room, every space he was ever in, never knowing whom he could trust and not fully trusting anyone. He could never sit with his back to the door. He always had to see what was coming and he was always ready to react. This is not something you can just shut off or snap out of.

A brotherhood had been formed between people of all walks of life with the men he had served with. There are no social boundaries in a brotherhood. It didn't matter how they felt about each other or if they would have been friends in a normal society. Their bond was for safety of the group above anything else. Everyone was needed. Everyone was there for a reason. He had been part of this amazing brotherhood who protected each other and were willing to die for each other. They were with each other every moment and in some ways they loved each other more than they loved themselves. They knew without a doubt they could always trust and count on each other even in death should they be the next one killed. Now all his brothers were scattered across the world. He was always wondering and worrying if his guys were okay. Without them close by he found himself feeling alone and vulnerable, not knowing who he could count on.

Will tried not to obsess about all the things that had happened but there was no way to keep it pushed down. When he was able to sleep it was always restless, if at all. The nightmares were unending and became even worse when it was hot or around certain dates of the year, of which there were many, especially when traumatic events had occurred in combat.

There are some things—especially in war—that are beyond horrible. They will never make sense and they will never be right no matter how much you talk about them. There is no point in trying to explain to someone who wasn't there what it was like. There are some things that you can't know or even come close to understanding unless you've actually been there. The majority of our society seems to think that talking about things makes them better. It's hard for them to understand that this is simply not always the case. Some things are beyond horrific and they always will be, and for some people talking about it, while it may be interesting for the listener, it is only a way of reliving it for the person who actually experienced it. There was no way for Will to articulate what he had been a part of and for a long time he didn't want to talk about it even if he could. He found himself feeling isolated and alone, surrounded by people who would never be able to comprehend or understand why he was the way he was.

Will was blessed with a very loving and supportive family. He was glad to be back near them and a part of their lives again, but he was unable to truly be honest with them because there were many things he was simply unable to talk about and also because he didn't want to cause them any more worry. The time he was away at war was hard enough on them. Now he had made it back alive and, on the outside, appeared to be in good health. He thought they deserved the peace of knowing he was okay and safe. Even though it was obvious to anyone who knew him that he had forever been changed, he still wanted to protect his loved ones from knowing just how bad it really was for him. He found himself back in a society of peers whose main stress was what grade they were going to get on their midterm. He was surrounded by an innocent and naive and seemingly oblivious society that went about their daily routines and normalcy of life sweating the small stuff like it mattered, just like he had done before war changed him and opened his eyes to a completely different reality.

But now he was back. While everything seemed to be, for the most part, the same as when he left, at the same time it wasn't at all the same and never would be because he was completely different. He now found himself not only struggling to function back in society but also was also faced with the big question of what are you going to do now. Will came back from war in his twenties when most people his age were just starting on their journey of trying to figure life out, but he had more miles on him than most old men. He had truly experienced life *and* death and had been prepared for his own death from a very young age. He somehow had survived against the odds and he came away from it with a real understanding and appreciation of how short and precious life is.

Will moved around a lot. He was always trying to keep busy and on the go, constantly looking for distractions to try to keep his mind from racing back to combat. Once you've been shot at or in a firefight, any other adrenaline rush doesn't even come close. One of the good things about an adrenaline rush is that your mind only thinks of what it needs to in order to survive. It's a moment that your mind is clear and you are able to be truly present in that moment and not think of anything else. It is also a great reminder of how life is good.

Will sought out adrenaline rushes quite often and spent as much time as possible skydiving and rock climbing. He was spending a lot of time in Eloy at Skydive Arizona. There had been a skydiver who had died and they had planted a tree in his honor. Will spent a lot of time out by that tree because it gave him a feeling of peace when he was near it. Quite often, he would sit by it and draw or write in his journal. One day, during a time when he was feeling completely lost, he went and lay down next to the tree, staring up at the sky and pleading in desperation for a sign to tell him what he was meant to do. War had taught him to believe that everything happens for a reason, that there is no such thing as a coincidence and to trust your gut. In that moment a helicopter flew directly over him and that tree and he knew that he was meant to be a helicopter pilot.

The bond Will had formed with his men in combat had taught him not to judge people before he learned their story and really got to know them for who they are. It taught him that everyone has something to offer and that you can learn something from every person if you approach them with an open mind and a willingness to learn and listen. Even through his private struggle he formed bonds and friendships with almost everyone he met all over the world. It was through the passing of time, reconnecting with his men and other veterans, the people he met and conversations he had, his open-minded approach to life and ideas, and his loving and supportive family and close friends that helped tip the scale and allow him to start his journey toward finding peace and living a happy and healthy life.

Having the goal to start school to become a helicopter pilot was something to work toward and direction for his life, and it helped him to get his footing. He felt that he owed it to his men to figure out how to process all that they had experienced in a healthy way so that they could all see that it was possible, through the Hippie, to live in peace. He was determined to lead by example. Will followed his gut and studied Aviation Science at Utah Valley University and earned his pilot's license.

There was no doubt that he had made the right decision. Will loved flying and he was an amazing pilot. There were few things in his life that made him feel more at peace than flying the helicopter and it turned out to be a major tool in his healing process. His experience and trauma from combat was always with him for the rest of his life, but flying had taught him that he could enjoy life again, that he didn't have to just go through the motions pretending. Flying was invigorating and it awakened his soul. For Will, it was as Leonardo da Vinci had said "...once you have tasted flight, you will forever walk the earth with your eyes turned skyward, for there you have been, and there you will always long to return."

Will had found his place where he truly belonged. The earth's magnificent landscape mingled with the infinite, the view from his office couldn't be beat. He became a flight instructor and worked hard to build his flight hours every chance he got. Will was very patient and a great teacher to all who were lucky enough to have him as an instructor. After years of financial struggle paying back his school debt and searching for every contract flight job he could find to build his experience, his hard work and dedication paid off and he eventually landed a career job as chief helicopter pilot for Lucas Oil. While flying for the Lucas Oil off road races, Will traveled throughout the country and had the opportunity to meet and connect with many more people. Everyone at the races seemed to know who he was. He was the helicopter pilot circling over the track as the videographer filmed the races, and he was also the one taking people up on the VIP helicopter rides before and after the race. It's hard not to notice *that* guy. Being a helicopter pilot is really cool. Pretty much every man alive has been in awe of helicopters since he was a little boy, and chicks just dig it.

But that wasn't what caused people to be drawn to Will. Often when you would overhear people talking about Will you would hear simply "Will is a great guy," "He's one of the good guys," "He's good people," "Salt of the earth." And he was. Will was a very casual laid-back guy with a light-hearted, boyish sense of humor. You would most likely see him in flip flops and a wrinkly shirt. His idea of getting dressed up was to throw his shirt in the dryer to get some of the wrinkles out. He could be described as scruffy, and his hands were often dirty from working hard and living life. He was a bit of a jokester and had a playful teasing side to him, but he was genuine and kind and simply good to the core. Even people who had just met him once felt a connection to him because he treated everyone like they mattered and were special, because to him every life was precious. It wasn't really anything specific that he did, it was just the way he made people feel.

Will's experience in war shaped him and completely changed him, but it didn't define who he was. He was lost for a long time in the darkness that war created inside of him. However, he was able to make it through and find a great deal of peace and have a healthy and optimistic outlook despite the hell he had been through. He found his balance by being true to himself, living his life to the fullest with his spirit of adventure, and not letting fear prevent him from fulfilling his dreams. But mostly he healed through helping other people.

Will was the kind of guy who would help anybody. Strangers were just friends he hadn't met yet. Whenever he saw someone who needed help he would drop whatever he was doing to help—whether it was helping a stranded motorist on the side of the road, helping a mom in the grocery store parking lot who had locked her keys in the car, or just being there for a friend who was going through a hard time. If you needed Will, you could always count on him to be there and to follow through until everything was okay.

Will loved his mom and his amazing family and friends, and he was a master at keeping in touch and letting you know that he cared. But he also cared for all people. When he learned of Biomass threatening the health and quality of life of the children and people of Jasper, Indiana he took it upon himself to do whatever he could do to help and raise awareness even though at first he knew no one in the town. Will's unending desire to help people was why he wanted this journal published. He believed even if it only helps one person then it was meant to be. His hope was that it would not only help other returning combat veterans know that they are not alone, but also that it might help family members or loved ones under-stand what it might have been like, that experiences in combat are not something that can be easily described, if at all. Sometimes, to understand that it simply "is what it is" is best and helps us to not take it personally when things are left unsaid.

On May 24, 2013, Will and his passenger set out on a routine VIP helicopter ride after the filming of the races that evening had concluded. When they did not return, a search party was sent out to discover that they had both tragically died when the helicopter he was flying crashed near Cross Timbers in Hickory County, Missouri.

Will was always safe. Whether he was on the ground or in the sky, he was always safe. He cared more about other people's safety than his own, and he was an incredibly skilled pilot. He was still a soldier in many ways because he would always protect and he would sacrifice himself for others. Those who knew Will know that he would have died a hundred times if it meant he could have saved his passenger. Our thoughts and prayers are always with her family and everyone who loves her because we also know the deep pain of losing such an irreplaceable beautiful soul who gave so much to this world just by being in it.

Will is a shining example that "life is good" and that it's possible to live a peaceful life even after war. A saying that he believed in and referred to quite often for a reminder in times of turmoil was "Peace. It does not mean to be in a place where there is no noise, trouble, or hard work. It means to be in the midst of those things and still be calm in your heart." After all, as Will often said, life without challenge is a farce.

Peace.

Lauren Hughes is a professional photographer and one of Will's closest friends.

THROUGH THE EYES OF MARK JONES
AND BRYAN MARACLE

THROUGHOUT HISTORY THERE ARE great men and women who are bridge builders between unlikely, and many times conflicting, groups of people; the kind of people who effortlessly cross between social boundaries and make lasting connections with everyone on the way. Will Higginbotham was one of these people.

As a fourth generation Arizona boy, Will's humble beginnings were spent growing up between Coolidge and Florence, Arizona, where mischief and adventure were a part of life. The desert cowboys that play and make mischief in the desert of south central Arizona kindled Will's spirit for adventure, while his mother implanted the understanding of loyalty and uncompromising love.

On the day he joined the US Army, Will and his Grandpa were talking about the Army and the advertisements that promoted helping you to "be all that you can be." Will laughed and said he wanted the army to make a man out of him. His Grandpa wisely said, "The army won't do that for you. You can choose to be a man or you can choose to be an asshole. It's your choice. You have to do it for yourself. The army can give you options to explore for your future, but ultimately, the choice to be a man is yours alone. No one can do it for you." That day, Will took his grandpa's advice to heart and determined he would do his best to be "the best that he could be."

As a soldier in the United States Army, Will's first assignment was in Alaska. After a winter of blood thickening cold he was encapsulated by a group of young adventure seekers who just wanted to climb, ski, hike, or paddle anything they could find. With this carefree group Will's *being* pivoted. In the space between mountain adventures and military training his balance of life began to form.

In 2003, the wilds of Alaska were augmented by the culture of Italy, when Will re-enlisted and began a three-year deployment with the 173rd Airborne Combat Brigade. This included two tours of duty, one in Iraq and one in Afghanistan. Being among the first paratroopers to land in Iraq, the realities of war started to become evident. Friends and family who knew him recall the shift very well and quickly came to understand the shed of innocence that war causes.

Returning to Italy, between the two wars, the adventures resumed, but the lens being used to find adventure was different. During the time between tours there was no shortage of adventures with climbing, drawing, spending time with the locals, and traveling Italy. This reinvigorated him with a greater appreciation for life, but his innocence was gone forever.

The return to civilized living was short-lived as he was quickly called for his second tour, this time in Afghanistan. *Chaos of War, Balance of Life* was a mechanism for grounding the struggles and internal conflict he experienced with war. As a team leader in a recon unit, the struggle to keep his spirit grounded was the inspiration for writing this journal. The challenge of war and love for his men precipitated from the love of his mother. He needed her to understand that her love would be forever evident in him, no matter how deep the scars of combat ran.

Like any great adventure, Will's journey through war was a life-changing event; as it is for all our service men and women. The war imprinted deep memories that only soldiers can truly understand. The transition from war to peace was Will's next great adventure. With the inward embrace of peace, the words uttered during an epic prewar adventure, "Its OK I am a pacifist," began to churn the ideals of what it meant to be a peaceful man and where his place in the world would be.

Shortly after his return home, the landing of a medevac helicopter at an accident triggered epic memories from the war. Acknowledging this as trauma, he decided to take it head on. He wrote:

Fear is what you have in your heart when you face what terrifies you. When you face this creature, you take it the same way it takes you, by using it's weakness against its self. When you defeat this fear you gain courage, faith, and pride. All these things combined are what makes you strong and give you strength and endurance to conquer that which plans to conquer you. God give me strength to do what it is I need to gain from my fear by using the trials I have made it through in the past, amen.

Will began to conquer his fear by piling his energy into his passions and finding what would be the opportunity for adventure for the rest of his life. In looking back at his trauma and his time in the military he realized he spent a lot of time riding in helicopters; in a moment he set his mind to using a source of his internal scares as a tool for healing. He was going to learn to fly helicopters. The decision led to uncovering his passion for flying. Quite often his Facebook posts would read "the view from my office," accompanied by a photo from the cockpit of the helicopter he was flying.

Famously, Will's experiences in the school of hard knocks became quotable Will-isms that began to radiate across the lips of family, friends, and fellow adventurers he touched after leaving the army. One of his more famous was when asked about the war and what it was like to be on the front lines he would compassionately repeat a phase he heard someone else say, that he had adopted as his own, "warring for peace is like whoring for virginity."

In each successive adventure the light and love instilled by his mother, family, and closest friends brought out the development of what was to become his mantra and most famous tag line for all that knew him, "Life is Good." These simple words became a mechanism that grounded him, and those around him, in a focus on the positive. To this day the transformation through aspiration is the spirit of his motto that still lives on through his family and friends.

As many returning veterans know, living the aspirations of "Life is Good" is not easy. The foundation of Will's healing journey lay in stepping back from the turmoil and taking time to learn a new vocation, which he loved. His healing process began by participation in counseling for treatment of PTSD. He took the skills he learned and added his own flair to the healing process by participating in activities that nurtured his soul. Will found this in continuing his journaling, art, flying, skydiving, yoga, camping, hiking, rock climbing, visiting hot springs, riding his motorcycle, listening to a wide range of music, and reconnecting with family, friends, and his brothers made in combat.

In one of his post war writings he shared:

I do have to live under the shadow of responsibility to my men. I cannot slip or let them slip. But with motivation . . . my present is more than tolerable for a couple, I think, good reasons. I got it in my head that without me and guys like me, a way of life would fade away. Someone has to protect the Camelot of today. Because I have a role in the defense of this beautiful nation, I like to think that I appreciate a little more than the next guy.

After four years of struggling with how to support himself by flying, the rewards of hard work and spreading good charma paid off. He landed his dream job with Lucas Oil in typical Will fashion: by telling the unfettered truth.

One day, when flying for a contractor, hired by Lucas Oil to capture aerial footage of the off road truck races, Will found himself sharing a cold beverage with the CFO of Lucas Oil. Will discussed with him and demonstrated that it was in their best interest to buy their own helicopter. Will's straight shooting honesty landed him the job as chief pilot at Lucas Oil and as usual he warmed the hearts of his coworkers and quickly became part of the Lucas Oil family. Through this new family he began forming close bonds and making lasting impressions on everyone he met.

Will was always willing to share his love of flying and the Lucas family encouraged him to share his passion by taking people on rides in the helicopter. His favorite was taking kids up in the air. He always made it into their personal adventure. Many friends and family cherish the memories of sharing rides and experiencing first hand Will's love of flying.

It wasn't until his passing that Will's loved ones realized just how wide and far reaching his adventurous, charismatic, and radiant personality reached. Thousands of people around the world were touched in a special way by knowing him. Through his life experiences Will gained wisdom far above his years. He put his leadership and friendship to work, connecting some of the most unlikely characters in humor, love, and a peaceful existence that rose from the realities of war. For Will, experiencing darkness was a means to see all the places light can be; because through God's light we find peace.

Will's journey of healing and search for peace evolved and brought a balanced serenity to the world he came into contact with. We hope that this journal will help readers seeking peace to see the possibilities for building their own space for balance in a world riddled with chaos.

With humility and a humble spirit we thank you for taking this journey and becoming among the many that strive to live the mantra "Life is Good." It is with strength and peace we share in paying our love forward.

Mark Jones and Bryan Maracle, close friends that taught Will to climb mountains in Alaska.

ACKNOWLEDGMENTS

AS WILL'S MOM, I want to express my thankfulness to:

God, for bringing Will home safely from the war and allowing us the privilege of having seven years with him before his death.

Jody Stone and Aaron Higginbotham for working with Will/me on the interior of the journal.

Peter Park, Jenny Baker, and Judy Worley for helping with pictures and punctuation.

Todd Vinne and Joey Leatham for helping to get permissions from those named in the book and providing insight into some of the writings.

Melissa and Regan Leuders: Time spent living with you after the war helped Will begin the journey toward finding healing in his heart.

The Felix Family: Hours spent at the Felix Ranch, especially hanging out with Josh (listening to music) or chatting with the other family members, helped to ground Will as he began to search for ways to reach his goal of becoming a pilot.

The Maracle family: who adopted Will as a family member and graciously allowed him to stay at their family home while he attended helicopter school. It was their love and prayers that helped him to focus on his spiritual development after the war.

The 173rd Airborne Brigade, 2-503rd, Scouts: You were instrumental in bringing Will safely home to us from the war. Because of you we had seven years with him after his return from war. We appreciate you and your service to our country more than words can say.

Thank you Dereck Huss, Todd Venne, Nolan Bousquet, Patrick Brannan, Joseph Leatham, Drew Linville, Jarrod Drake, Nick Conlon, Scott Sprague, Thom Wojo, Nick Pack, and Ryan Workman—for coming to Arizona to support us during Will's Memorial Service. Your presence there meant everything to us. He called you brothers. We are very proud of each of you and your service to our country.

Bryan, Mark, and Lauren: Thank you for writing the Afterwords.

Lucas Oil: You allowed Will to pursue his passion for flying, and you paid him for it. You also welcomed him to California and helped him feel at home there. Thank you.

My husband and children: Tim, Heather, Stephanie, and Aaron — without my family, and their love and support, this journal project could not have been completed.

All of Will's other close friends and relatives: Your calls, sharing of stories about his life, and encouragement while we pursued the publishing of his journal have touched us deeply.

Last but not least:

Thank YOU for reading this journal. We hope it has helped you in some way.

My son's wishes were that the profits from this journal would be shared with "War heroes and not war makers." In keeping with those wishes, we have chosen the Open hands Outreach Program (OHOP) http://ohopcharity.org/ in Coolidge Arizona to share in the profits from this book. OHOP supports veterans and their families in the community where Will grew up.

Life is good.

Peace.